AN AMERICAN SAVAGE
in a
FRENCH HOTEL

An Accurate Accounting of the Various Reasons
I Should Be Hung

Darryl Mockridge

This book is dedicated to my very dear wife, who suffers more greatly than I, but has chosen to bear it with dignity.

This is not a work of fiction. It was originally published, in 2010, as TRIAL BY GUEST, by Henry Edward Fool. Names have been changed of course, not that any of us are ever capable of recognizing ourselves.

ESTUARY PUBLICATIONS
© 2019 estuarypublications.com
Grass Valley, California
ISBN: 9781699858257

CONTENTS

Mockridge

INTRODUCTION (you can probably just skip this)

I'm a desk clerk in a small privately-owned hotel, and that's an awkward situation for me because, fundamentally I'm an inward—and by that I mean socially inept—individual. Dealing with strangers on a daily basis is not just difficult for me—demanding an exuberance for my fellow man which I simply do not possess—it is slightly painful at times, at times embarrassing. And, because I have a very low tolerance for either idiocy or pretense, sometimes it becomes almost unbearable.

With my slightly misanthropic tendencies, my general disregard for authority of any sort, my contrary nature, my apparent arrogance—which shields a genuine fundamental shyness—and my driving desire just to be left alone (with my wife, a cello, a dog, a cat, a few books) for long, prolonged, and extended periods, the "hospitality industry" is the very worst possible business for me to find myself in. There is no doubt about that.

It would be difficult to find any man less suited to the task of welcoming people warmly.

It's natural, I think, at this point, for you to ask how I managed to get into this situation. I've gnawed on that so many times that I've shattered teeth in the process, but that will be explained in time. The mystery is how I remain. Why FATE should waste so much effort keeping me in this utterly hopeless, painful and senseless situation, I cannot guess. Clearly the gods have taken a real disliking to me.

May I say quickly here that Will Rogers was an idiot. He's the one who famously declared, "I never met a man I didn't like." It would be impossible for me to count all the people I've met with whom I want nothing to do whatsoever. If I could choose the people I have contact with, first would be my delightful wife, and after that the list would be very short indeed. Yet, I find myself surrounded every minute of every day with strangers.

To complicate things, my defenses are such that many of these strangers, guests at this hotel, believe that I am something which I am not; that I am cold or arrogant, or that I am indifferent to their needs, that I don't like people in general, or, worst of all perhaps, that I am French. None of that is true.

At any rate, true or not, our guests are not all immediately enthralled with me—some seem to develop an almost immediate disliking to me—and because of that I live under constant reproach. When a guest is dissatisfied, my name is very often attached to their complaint; but that's because, when there is a problem, I'm the one most likely to respond to their call. So, *my name and face then become closely associated with their discontent.* Whatever the cause of it, I believe their distaste for me is largely a psychological matter, and largely their own.

Until you've read more, if you can, please just accept this as fact: many people checking into a hotel have needs far above and beyond a nice, clean, comfortable and safe place to sleep. I've had years of experience in this business and I know what I'm talking about.

Many people checking into a hotel have extraneous needs, and, whenever those needs aren't met, it's the staff's fault.

They have a point of course when one of those needs is for the constant reassurance that they are superior beings and it becomes our job to supply that assurance by professing our own inferiority through both word and gesture, whenever we find ourselves in their presence. I have to admit that I either can not or will not make any effort to fulfill this need in any guest, and the more glorious they are, the less I am willing to contribute to the illusion. You can probably see already how that might lead to trouble.

What's unfair about that arrangement (and I speak only for myself here, not for the hundreds of thousand of hotel and restaurant employees throughout the world who know exactly what I am talking about) is that I am only allowed to express my feelings about such guests through a somewhat brittle courtesy; guests however may express their displeasure with me through long scathing, rambling diatribes, riddled with childish vindictiveness and incised with great force into stacks of cheap, pastel-colored, personalized stationary with winged hearts in the corners, and mail all of that still-steaming vitriol, in matching envelopes, directly to my boss. It is amazing how many see that option and seize upon it. This book is, in part, my defense to some of the accusations found in such letters.

It would only disrupt the flow of things for me to say here that many people, many guests actually, enjoy doing business with me and that some guests have, over the years, become good friends. So I won't do that.

Nor will I slow things down by stopping here to say that my wife, who knows me best, thinks of me as a thoughtful, kind, and somewhat goofy guy who is generally good-natured and not too rarely in a good mood.
(I wanted to be absolutely sure of that statement, and, after checking with her, I feel comfortable letting it stand.)

Before you pass judgment on the matter however, let me first *ask* you something and then, let me *tell* you something.

Here's the question:
Are you in a position where every waking moment of every day, wherever you go and whatever you may be doing, you are likely to bump into complete strangers who expect you to treat them as if there could be no greater joy on earth than for you to run into them at that very moment?
That's the question.
I ask you this because that's my situation.

Now, the thing I'd like to *tell* you is: The average length of ownership of a *bed & breakfast* is 5 years, 2 months.

Let me explain. That means that people who consider themselves *gregarious*; who go about every day chirping joyously about how much they *just love people*; who, for as long as they can remember have hoped and prayed and yearned, and planned and plotted and saved; and pleaded in all earnestness with pure, aching, innocent hearts for the chance to—if God grants wishes—find themselves in the hospitality business (breathe here) after a few years of it, want nothing more sincerely than to GET OUT of the hospitality business.

People who make their living selling B&Bs rarely tout that fact in their chirpy little seminars however. They never tell their victims that it will take nearly as long to off-load one of those frilly little nightmares as it takes to discover that dealing with guests every nagging minute of every miserable day of their rapidly ebbing lives is not the dream they had once supposed it would be. That's a very carefully guarded, unspoken truth. And, if you multiply that truth by 100 or 1000 you begin to understand the small privately-owned hotel business.

Notes to the 2019 edition:

Things have changed a great deal in the ten years since an edict was issued declaring that I would no longer be allowed in the front office; only remarkable forbearance on the owner's part can explain why that decree wasn't issued years earlier. It would be ridiculous of me not to admit that.

So, I'm guessing things must be much better now, without me in the office. However, I cannot imagine that guests have changed much since then.

Mockridge

HOW I GOT INTO THIS AWKWARD POSITION

One afternoon, one of this hotel's best desk clerks (young, beautiful, charming, chirpy, and exceedingly French) was observed in the appalling, completely unacceptable act of insisting that a guest admit to the truth. I forget the details, or maybe I never knew the details, it hardly matters, but the scene was interesting because in this business the guest may not always be right, but *we,* the staff, are *always* wrong. Always. Whenever one of these matters goes to trial before the owner, things like facts, truth, and reality are never allowed to stand in the way of a swiftly delivered guilty verdict. We are all, each and every one of us, guilty from the moment we are hired.

When I arrived at the office, there was already a noticeable chill in the atmosphere. The opening shot had been fired, and the smoke still hung in the air. The desk clerk, Odile, was seated behind the desk and the guest was very properly seated, ramrod straight, across from her; they were glaring at each other in silence. The guest held her purse clenched in her lap as if Odile's next move might be to quickly lean over the desktop and snatch it. The deafening silence in that room was soon to change.

Somewhere in there, during the ice cold silence of the check-out process, the guest felt compelled to tell Odile—apparently yet again—that she had been mislead by something which Odile had said. In response, Odile denied having ever said it. The guest, assuming that Odile was restrained by her position as mindless and spineless servant to the hotel, demanded that she confess to having said this

thing—whatever it might have been. Odile not only
refused to admit it, she went so far as to correct the guest.
"I never told you that, Madame," she said flatly.
The tone of that statement got my attention.

At this point the guest's beady little eyes began to narrow
as she sensed something less than the anticipated boot-
licking subservience which one might normally expect
from a lowly desk clerk, and things soon escalated. The
guest stood up abruptly, saying, "You told me..." Odile
stood up on her side of the desk just as quickly and cut her
off by saying, "That is not true, Madame, and you know it
is not true."

The guest then fled the office while shouting over her
shoulder, "You said it. Admit it."
Odile followed her out into the hallway shouting, "That is
not true, Madame."
"Admit it," screeched the guest without looking back.
"No, you are wrong, Madame. I never told you that."
The guest stopped with her hand on the front door, wheeled
and shouted, "You said...", but seeing Odile in close
pursuit, escaped outside without finishing the thought.
Odile, while dashing down the hallway, was shouting,
"That is not true, Madame. You are wrong Madame." She
actually followed the guest outside onto the sidewalk and
was heard shouting out there, "That is not true, Madame!"
as the guest, successfully routed, scurried away.

The owner had long since emerged from his office to find
out what all the shouting was about, and we stood there in
the hallway together awaiting Odile's return from her

crusade. I had a barely restrained grin on my big stupid face. The owner, I noted, did not. What I saw as an act of heroism, he saw only as the willful breaking of convention.

When Odile returned she went stomping into our office with the owner following her. He was furious and had a lot of things to say to her in cold, subdued tones. She had my complete approval however; I was practically giggling with delight. In my mind, she was the one true champion of a very good and too-long neglected cause. Like Odile, I don't always thoroughly enjoy guests treating us as though they might have been royalty in some previous life and now recognize us in this one as the foul ingrate peasants who once sullenly tended their generously overflowing fields. Even less do I enjoy it when they think nothing has changed from that life to this.

So, I was delighted to see someone other than myself reject the universally accepted concept that humiliation of the staff is simply part of any good hotel experience. Fresh sheets, clean towels, full breakfast, talk down to the maid; insult the desk clerk on your way out the door…an excellent stay…I'd recommend this place to anyone. But, in this case, battle lines had been drawn, and I think *we* may have won that little skirmish. The enemy had certainly been driven from the field of battle.

The owner called Odile into his office, and shortly (by French standards) she returned to the front office to pick up her purse, slam a few drawers around, grab her coat, and make her way, head nicely tilted upward, out the door, never to be seen or heard from again.

As Odile was gathering her things, I told her, "I don't know what that was about, I don't even know if you were right, but I certainly applaud your spirit." I smiled.

Odile looked at me in that way the French look at anyone who doesn't speak French and expelled a puff of air, dismissing me entirely. She didn't want and certainly didn't need any American's approval. Just as a note: I'm sure Odile would want me to make it clear right here that she was not fired from the hotel, she quit. She quit with the kind of drama that we all dream of bringing to our quitting. Her departure was glorious. She looked great.

Of course, though the guest may not have been right, Odile was clearly very wrong, and, as said, guilty from the day she was hired. So, she had to go. But, she'd stood up against the ridiculous tyranny that some guests feel they have the right to impose upon the hotel staff, and won. In my view Odile was driven out by her own heroism.

Odile, wherever you are today, I salute you.

So, that's the how and the why of me moving suddenly from *night guy* to the front office at the hotel; there was no way on such short notice the owners could have avoided it.

My elevation would be the first time in many many many years any front desk clerk at the hotel didn't speak French; I would be the first American to ever hold that esteemed position. (And now, drawing from the owners' experience with me, it is very likely that I will be the last.) So, my bounce up the ladder meant that we needed a new night guy, and simple as the task might appear, it was not easy to find someone. Not everyone is cut out to be night guy at a small, privately owned hotel. I was. In fact, it can be reasonably argued that I was suited perfectly for the task.

And, not that it matters, but, I was happy as a night guy.

LUMBERJACK

To fill in the immediate gap, one of the French waiters was enrolled as the night guy. I don't know how this came about—whether he was asked or ordered to or volunteered —but on the first night he appeared at the front door to the hotel, ready, willing, perhaps a little too eager, apparently able, and dressed like a lumberjack. Why the lumberjack attire, neither my very dear good future wife nor I, her lucky future husband, could figure out, but there he was. He had on a plaid shirt, jeans, wide suspenders and heavy work boots. Should any trees need felling in the wee hours, we had our man already on site.

The first night that I had arrived for that same job, a year or two earlier, I was wearing respectable cotton twill pants, a reasonably expensive knit shirt (alligator, not rider with mallet) and the most expensive shoes I'd ever purchased in my life, since by that time I already knew the owner had a thing for shoes which could be defined almost entirely by the phrase: "a revulsion for sneakers". I wanted to make a good impression. I came prepared to escort guests arriving like thieves in the night to their room with some slight dignity.

On my first night as night guy, the owner himself was there to meet me when I arrived, and he asked me if I understood my task.
"Well," I said, "I'm here to assure the general security of the building; to let those *in* who belong here; to keep those who do not belong here *out*; and, overall, to represent the hotel to any guests who may require our attendance during

the night." The owner seemed somewhat startled by this response and, after some thought, approved it with a nod. (Just a note: I have never seen that nod of approval since.)

He then told me where I might find various things; he showed me the house phone, the security intercom, the video monitors, and he said this: "I can not insist, of course, but I strongly suggest that you get some sleep during the night. I think you will find this couch most accommodating. I have slept on it myself many long nights. What I am trying to tell you is that you are not expected to sit here in the office all night long, wide awake, bristling in anticipation of some event which will never occur." He pointed again at the leather couch in the lobby and laughed to himself, "We are old friends that couch and I." He sighed. "In the morning," he said, "if you wish, please go down to the restaurant, OUR restaurant, and have a good breakfast before you leave for wherever it is you go."

These were perhaps the kindest words the man has ever spoken to me. I say perhaps because I also seem to recall that on the first day I arrived to work at the front desk— after Odile's glorious departure—he said to me, "Oh, you can't go to work just like that; come down and have a little cup of coffee with us, and let us get to know one another. Why not?" he encouraged, "One must be *properly* nourished to undertake the tasks that manning the desk requires."

We did in fact go downstairs and had a little cup of good coffee, but I don't think we really got to know each other. Now of course, it's too late for that; each of us is convinced that he knows the other far too well, and much much more than either of us would truly care to.

When the little waiter arrived on his first night as night guy he asked my future wife where the pillows were and if she would leave a note instructing one of the maids to bring him a cup of fresh coffee first thing in the morning. His hope, he said, was that he could enjoy his coffee *before* going down to breakfast.

The following morning he complained bitterly that he had found the comings and goings of people during the night "very disturbing" and that he'd had "a difficult night." Those were his words. By the time he arrived for his second night's work he had come up with a plan to eliminate these small annoyances. He asked the owner's wife if he could simply unfold one of the roll-away beds in the linen room and set an alarm clock. I think at this point it became clear that the man did not entirely understand the nature of his job. Madame said quietly to her husband, "We might as well pay him to sleep at home in his own bed." I think the little waiter would have accepted such an arrangement providing that the compensation was suitable and the hotel also paid to have coffee delivered, before breakfast.

The night following the little waiter's dismissal my wife-to-be, whose job it became by default, was disturbed in the middle of the night by a person she described, in her own charming way, in socially acceptable but somewhat disapproving terms which the rest of us might translate loosely as "looking like a common whore".

This person insisted upon seeing *the night guy*. Apparently, this person had somehow become involved with *the night guy* on the previous evening and he had something of hers which she wished to recover. I didn't like hearing this and for the following few nights, until we could get someone to replace the lumberjack, I was both night guy and part time fill-in desk clerk.

During my first night back, an unwashed and in large part toothless little creature, with clownish make-up, a matted blonde wig and clothes which were two sizes too small for her, rang the doorbell looking for the night guy. I told her that I was the night guy. She told me, "No, THE night guy. Johnny. Where's Johnny?" I told her that Johnny had gone, and she said that he had something of hers. I asked her what it might be, and she told me that maybe it had gotten lost on the couch or under the couch or behind the couch. I winced. Then, she thought for a bit and said, "Or it could have been in that room in the back, where all the sheets are stacked up." I may have raised my eyebrows at this point, if they weren't already in the full upright position. I ran her off of course, but she had given me plenty to think about.

For the next several nights, she came back every couple of hours or so, and leaned on the doorbell until I came charging out of the lobby like a wounded bear. Then, after giving me the finger or sticking her abnormally tiny tongue out at me, she ran off. For this I found myself unforgiving of the little waiter. By what peculiarity of my own weak nature I can not say, but I liked that whorish looking little woman less each time she rang the doorbell.
I'm just that kind of guy.

But, what kind of human being am I after all, who can not put up with the relentless nightlong playful little pranks of a two-bit whore? This is a character flaw of mine. For this inflexibility I suppose I should shrug on the old noose and step off into the void.

THE NEXT NIGHT GUY

The next night guy the owner hired was a short, fat, very red-faced, extraordinarily red-faced, beet-faced, wheezy kind of fellow who spoke with a lisp. I don't know what his credentials were or where he came from, nor do I know why he was hired. On the first night, he arrived two minutes before his shift was to begin; I explained things to him and left him sitting behind the desk while I visited with my wife-to-be and we watched the end of an old movie.

When I was leaving I went by the front desk and saw that the new night guy had his head down on the desk, and was snoring. Since it was just a little after midnight I thought it would be fair to the establishment to wake him up; I thought the hotel should get a little more than an hour's attentiveness out of anyone claiming eight hour's work. So I stood in front of the desk and I cleared my throat. There was no response.
I said, "Hey."
There was no response.
I clapped my hands and, employing my very best imitation of an annoyed high school girl, said, "Excuse me!" and there was no response.
I shouted "HEY!" with no response from the man.

I had to admire his ability to sleep so deeply. I slammed both fists down on the surface of the desk, one on each side of his big red face, and there was no response. I began to doubt that the heavy breathing and loud snoring which emanated from the guy were actually indications of life.

"Hey!" I shouted again and, grabbing the edge of the desk, I gave the thing a shake, rattling it with all of my, now waning but once considerable, strength.

He looked up at me and rubbed his reddish eyes.
"Yeah?"
"They're not paying you to sleep," I said.
"How do you know what they're paying me to do?"
"I'm the guy who talked to you about what's expected of you. I'm the guy who showed you what to do, remember? I've done this job myself; I know what it entails."
He said nothing. He placed his head back down and very quickly fell into a deep sleep.

Almost a minute. That's the time I stood there completely astonished. It was not the first time that I thought this hotel could easily supply some clever young writer with all the elements necessary for an endless series of seemingly contrived but utterly true bizarre tales.

On this gentleman's second night I waited for his arrival and sometime after midnight (one hour after he was scheduled to start) I received a phone call from him. There was music in the background and, from the sounds that reached me, he held a cat upon his fat lap. I know cats and I know what it sounds like when they bump their bony little heads against a telephone handset, and I also know purring when I hear it.

He said, "I'm going to be late; I'm on BART and the train has broken down. So, I'm gonna be a little late."
He arrived a little after 2.

On this gentleman's third night, he didn't show up at all.

The following evening, during my shift at the front desk, he called to say, "Listen to me. I want the money you owe me sent to my home address, and I want it done immediately! Otherwise," he warned. "I've been known to cause trouble." I was digesting this in silence when he repeated himself. "I want the money, and I want it sent here immediately!" he shouted. Then he hung up.

I gathered from the somewhat aggressive nature of this demand that he'd been told that his services would no longer be needed at the hotel. Which meant, once again, that unless I stepped into the breach my dear wife-to-be would have to.

ANTOINE

Next was Antoine, a young Frenchman who impressed everybody on staff with his intelligence, reasonable good looks, the manner in which he presented himself, his eagerness to work and his quiet good-natured demeanor. The first night, I gave him instruction and was myself impressed. He seemed to have an immediate grasp of everything I said, both of the procedures and what was expected of him. By the second night, he seemed to understand a bit less though, and I recall marking that up as normal for anyone on their second day at work. The third night he came across as a complete idiot. There's really no other way to express it. He no longer knew how to do any of the things I'd explained, no matter how simple.

On the fourth night, from all indications, he wanted very much to make it perfectly clear that he honestly did not care. He'd had enough. He was through. He would go through the paces, but he wouldn't like it. It did not matter what was expected of him or what we thought of him. He also wanted us to know that his presence was a challenge to anybody who thought they might attempt to expel him. All of this was conveyed without a word.

It had been a quick and somewhat startling transition from golden boy to entrenched belligerent. Even people who work in government put in a couple of solid weeks' work before they start fuming and taking actions which openly demonstrate their utter disdain for their employment. (I'm just guessing.)

At this point, the owner was so desperate to have someone, anyone, on duty at night that our reports on this mal-metamorphosis, from savior to oozing sore on prom night, were simply brushed away. It was one of those rare moments when I could see the man's point of view. After all it was better having a smoldering malcontent on board than either a puffy red-faced lunkhead sleeping like a log or a wayward waiter dallying with bottom-of-the-barrel whores and performing unimaginable acts in the lobby or linen room, in exchange for a few laughs, humiliation and the degradation of all humanity. From my point of view, it was certainly better to have Antoine in place than for either my future wife or myself to be stuck with the position.

On or about the fifth night I passed by the office to see how Antoine was doing and discovered that he was doing quite well. He was leaning back in a chair with his sneaker enwrapped feet up on the desk, and he had the largest stainless steel bowl obtainable from our kitchen on his lap, and in it was what must have been two gallons of ice cream. The ice cream was covered with nuts and drenched in our own expensive, hand-wrought, chocolate sauce. When I asked him how things were, he nodded enthusiastically and raised his spoon toward the heavens. His mouth was too full to speak, but not too full to grin like the villainous unshaven scoundrel that he was.

On night six, after the pastry chef had discovered the missing ice cream, Antoine was sullen. He asked me if I would supply him with a key to the refrigerator. I didn't even know that the refrigerator had a key—until that very day none of them had ever been locked before.

On night seven, I passed Antoine in the office on my way to my future wife's rooms and he glared at me. Sylvie took me quickly inside, locked both locks, and breathlessly told me that Antoine was not happy.
Actually, I had already guessed that.

Apparently he had come into the hotel that afternoon and cornered the pastry chef, and demanded a key to the refrigerators and freezers. Now, the pastry chef—to whom you have not been introduced—is nobody you want to mess with, whether you've been introduced or not. She is 4 foot 9 and weighs a mere 83 pounds, but you don't want to mess with her—believe me. The chef, who is one foot taller and 200 pounds heavier, and who knows her better than anyone else at the hotel, does not mess with her. So, Antoine did not get his key. Apparently, Antoine had been stomping around in the hallways, pacing back and forth like a cage-crazed animal, ever since the confrontation. The story about him carving the words ice cream into his own forehead is just that, a story. As is the tale of him smashing the freezer lock with a sledge hammer…he used a bolt cutter.
I instructed Sylvie to lock the door as soon as I left that night, and not to unlock it until Antoine was well gone in the morning.

When I passed by the office, on my way out, I looked in. He was stretched out with his feet up on the desk again but with nothing to eat and nothing to say to me.
"Is everything OK?" I asked.
"What does this matter to you?" (If he had had a cigarette dangling from his disdainfully curled lip that would have been a nice touch…but he didn't.)

"Well, if something is wrong," I said, "you can talk to me about it."

"What makes this any of your business?"

"Well, I have some say around here, and if you…"

"Why don't you just leave," he said, and he got up and slammed the office door in my face.

This went on for some time, Antoine's discontent growing exponentially, becoming more undeniable with every passing day, until it was expansive enough to wiggle its way under the owner's office door and crawled up and settled in his lap with bared fangs. The following day there was a little get-together with the owner and Antoine in his office and, as if by magic, Antoine was suddenly no longer in the hotel's employ. This was a relief for everybody on staff. Here was a man, disgruntled if not dangerous, who had *keys to everything* in the place—except the freezer where we kept our precious ice cream. "If anything ever happens," I told Sylvie, "climb into one of those freezers. It's the only safe place in the joint."

The following day—the day after Antoine was dismissed—Sylvie and I went out for a little walk and there was an old van parked in our passenger loading zone, and in it, smoking a cigarette and staring at us sullenly, was Antoine. For almost two weeks Antoine and his van were parked out in front of the hotel, day and night, twenty-four hours a day, until one day, POOF! it was no longer there. Somehow that gave me the creeps. Not seeing that van parked out front worried me as much as seeing it there; now I began to wonder where it was, what he was planning, and when he might suddenly reappear.

I am sorry to have to report that the day after Antoine was dismissed the owner acted in a very American manner. By this I mean he took immediate action. There was none of the usual deep, passionate, heart-wringing discussion that dragged on for months and involved every French-speaking person residing either in the hotel or in distant lands. He simply had the front door lock re-keyed.

This is how quickly it happened: The owner spoke to the kid, asked him to leave, and, BAM, like that, the front door locks were being changed. As the locksmith departed I thought I could hear the proverbial sigh of relief coming simultaneously from every single person on staff, now cowering safely inside the hotel.

IRREPLACEABLE ME

After Antoine's not so sudden disappearance there arrived, as if by miracle, a young Italian. He spoke English with the delightful flexibility and eager fluency of a six year-old, and his accent gave everything he said a kind of cheerful idiotic charm. I instructed him as to the nature of the job and he launched into it with bubbly enthusiasm. He did his job well and he did it well for something like six or eight weeks. Then he departed for a brief vacation, back home in Italy.

He told us that he would be gone for a week, but emailed us later, from Italy, to say it would be two weeks instead. Then he emailed us again to say it would be a month, and then…we never heard from him again.

I think somewhere about that time Sylvie and I were married and the night guy thing fell, as a kind of wedding gift to us, once again into my lap. So, then I was both desk clerk and night guy… as I am still today. Ah well, that which does not kill us makes us hopelessly depressed, irritable, and maybe just a little justifiably snappish.

Oh and here's something of note: after this nice young Italian departed, all the computers in the place began to freeze up sporadically, and not in the usual way but with an impressive stubbornness (control/alt./delete did **nothing**.) While they were being re-instated, re-configured and coaxed back into action, we discovered that someone had (perhaps inadvertently) visited and subsequently subscribed to every pornographic site in the internet universe.

We further discovered that most, if not all of these visits had taken place, by coincidence I'd imagine, between 11 PM and 6 o'clock in the morning. The owner, when he heard of this, shrugged and—being French—declared dryly, "C'est normal!"

If so, it was the only normal thing associated with the hotel's night guy replacement efforts.

But that's neither here nor there. I was back and, though it remains officially unrecognized to this day, apparently I am irreplaceable. More accurately maybe I should say at least I can't be replaced by a part-time whoring, French lumberjack; I can't be replaced by a fat, belligerent, red-faced liar who sleeps like the dead; I can't be replaced by a young Frenchman who, though he appears normal at first, turns out to be stark raving mad and potentially dangerous. And I can't be replaced by a good natured young Italian with a limited English vocabulary but an unlimited hunger for pornography. I'm sure this would not be recognized as a significant scientific sample, but that's the way I summed it up for my wife, and she agreed.

Not everybody is cut out for night guy at this small, privately-owned, French hotel.

EMERGENCY DEFINED

During her brief stay here one young French student, an intern at the hotel named Sophie, was asked to fill in as *night guy* for a few days so that my very dear wife and I might get away for a bit. She was an interesting kid; she genuinely liked every person she met, and they all responded appropriately. Because she was black and because she had that unsinkable attitude, I once asked her about racism; I wanted to know how someone with such buoyancy handled it. But, then I had to explain racism to her, because she claimed to have never experienced such a thing. So she was much more than just an interesting kid. Not having been raised in the United States she had never been taught to see herself as a perpetually downtrodden victim, and consequently lived a remarkably joyful life.

One time I came in to find her slouched lazily in one of the office chairs doing a fairly impressive imitation of me, which seemed to entertain Sylvie enormously. She kept repeating the same phrases over and over: "There is no end to it." and "Why in the name of God…" and something else which I forget, none of which, as far as I could recall, had ever come from these lips. When I protested, they both laughingly proclaimed that such statements were the very essence of my being. She was a good kid, but she had me confused with someone else.

The three nights she sat in for me proved so eventful that she begged never to have to work nights again. On the first night a nice older gentleman appeared before her at the beginning of her shift and asked if she could help him remember what room he was in. She discovered that he was in #508 and kindly showed him to his room. Several minutes later he appeared again and asked if she could help him find his room. She told him nicely that it was #508. She kindly showed him to #508. When he appeared before her a third time, she told him, she showed him. Nicely. Kindly. With patience. And it went on like that for several hours; after a while he'd appear, she'd tell him the room number and show him to his room. And although she recognized, as anyone would, that this gentleman had a problem, despite her sympathetic nature, after a certain amount of this, the glimmer of our true nature began to glow within the young French intern, and she was no longer delighted to see him. I know this because she admitted as much to me. But, because Sophie was a far better person than some of the rest of us, she made it through that night without strangling the poor old fellow to death in the hallway and tucking the body quietly away in a maid's closet.

Due to my passive memory I had to be reminded by my good wife that somewhere in the midst of this ongoing circus Sophie became so flustered that she opened the wrong door, walking in on some people creating their own entertainment. I don't know how that adds anything to the tale however and so, you won't read about it here.

The very next night, things seemed quiet by comparison, until sometime after 3 A.M. when sirens on the street awoke her and kept her awake with the accompanying flashing red lights. When a fire truck stopped directly in front of the hotel, she got up to peek through the lace curtains and see what the matter was. Almost instantly there was a loud commotion at the front door as firemen, instead of ringing the bell, tried to bust their way through. She let them in and, as they charged by, one of them demanded, "How do we get to room #307?" Dashing up the stairs just ahead of them, she showed them to room #307. They were eager to break down that door too—too much training, not enough action, I suppose—until she squeezed in front of them and opened it with her pass key. They shoved her aside and rushed in to discover that there was nobody in there.

There was nobody in the room, in the closet, in the bathroom or under the bed. "Where is the woman who is supposed to be in this room?" Sophie did not know. Emergency Medical Technicians arrived on the scene only seconds after and there was some discussion about the absence of this woman. There was a group shrug and, turning as a group, they all went clumping down the winding steps to the ground floor shrouded in a cloud of disappointment.

As the firemen were going out, a young woman was coming in. She looked at the crowd on the sidewalk and asked, "Wow, what's happening?"
Sophie told her, "Someone called 911 to say the woman in #307 needs help."
"Really? I'm in #307."
"Did you call 911?"
"No. I wasn't even here."
Sophie was naturally mystified…as was the woman herself, as were the firemen when one of them overheard it, as were

the EMTs when that information was conveyed to them, as was everyone standing on the sidewalk in the middle of the night, who heard the tale and passed it on.

The departure of the firemen and EMTs was somewhat less dramatic than their arrival, slower and a great deal less noisy. Sophie told us a 'weird energy' lingered in the hallway for a while after they'd all gone.

The following evening, the woman in #307 returned from a wedding reception, came into the office, and laughingly explained that she had figured it out.

She had been scheduled to take photographs at the wedding reception. While checking her gear the night before, she'd discovered that the batteries to her camera were dead. She called her sister to ask if she could pick up some batteries for her on the way to the reception. Her sister was out at the time, so, she left a message on her answering machine: "Please help me! Call me back immediately. I really need your help. This is an emergency!" The sister got home very late—pre-wedding jitters—picked up the message, called the hotel where the switchboard, now closed, put her through to the room automatically. There was no answer.

She tried not to panic, but waited a very reasonable four to seven minutes before calling again. When there was no answer again, she chewed things over a bit. What were the options? Let's see… her sister could be… dead. That's ridiculous; she's probably just… dead. OR, well, of course, she could be… so seriously injured she could not answer the phone; there was at least some hope in that.

That was her frantic thinking as she listened to the ringing on the other end of the line, before panicking and calling 911. Meanwhile her sister, very much alive and unable to sleep, from worrying about those batteries, had gone out to look for a 24 hour drugstore.

That night was eclipsed on the very next evening, when a nicely-aging, naked French blonde disrupted things by sprinting by the office and shouting, in French, "STOP THAT MAN… Stop him.' Just ahead of her ran a fully clothed man lugging a suitcase. He ran out the door and into the street. Sophie, inspired by comic books, sprang into action. Being young and fleet of foot she actually collared the man about half way down the block and held him there until the naked French lady arrived.

At that point, because of the confrontation that ensued, certain things started to become clear. The first was that Sophie would have to, for the sake of decency, offer the French woman her sweater. The second was that the man had not stolen the suitcase.

As they shouted at each other, there in the street, in the middle of the night, in French, it all came out. The man was the woman's boyfriend. Accusations that he had been 'hitting on' her teenaged daughter—who occupied the adjoining room—had reached that point where no honest man could, in good conscience, any longer remain. For some reason, a secret late night departure seemed the only solution for him. The only solution for her, when she opened one eye and saw him tip-toeing out the door with his suitcase, was to set chase.

Though the owner proclaimed this naked French woman to be one of his favorite guests of all time, commending her for her great passion, she had been the final straw for Sophie. Three nights was enough for her. She just wasn't cut out for working nights at the hotel.

But, I make a peculiar judge in the matter; I'm not cut out to work in the light of day.

A BRIEF INTRODUCTION TO GUESTS

The word *guest* does not carry embedded within its simple construct any indication of royalty, although many guests seem to think it's the very root of the word. There are words for persons of a high regal stature, but guest is not one of them. The Olde English form of the word *guest* simply means *stranger,* and the Latin form means *enemy*, both of which conform perfectly to my understanding of it, as gathered through years of personal experience. While we're at it, under any interpretation, the term, *desk clerk* does not imply either idiocy or simpering servitude.

I wanted to straighten that up because some of the people who walk through our door here at the hotel seem unclear on the definition of these terms.
So, now the rest of us can move on.

For anyone not working in the hotel business I want to tell you that many guests seem to have a very real need for something; I've never really determined exactly what. They are needy at any rate, and their hope seems to be that their stay at the hotel will provide them with an opportunity to fill-in whatever it is they lack in their lives beyond these sheltering walls. If the nature of this 'neediness' is unclear to you, that's OK, it remains unclear to me, and I've been in this business for a very long weary time. It is always this undefined need that turns an otherwise anodyne guest into a nightmarish guest.

There are many good guests, but those arrows that *missed* Sebastian provided him with no opportunity for sainthood.

It was through suffering those bolts which tore his flesh and embedded themselves deep within that he gained his martyrdom, his magnificence, his beatification.

Among the *good guests* there are the somewhat-less-than-good guests. They make up perhaps as much as 25% of all guests, and whatever else they may be, they are, from all indications, helpless. So, although they may be good people—neither rude nor unbearable—they are not ideal guests. The hotel is here, of course, to serve its guests, not to serve its staff, so I'm restrained from mentioning St. Sebastian again.

With this in mind, hoteliers, drawing upon centuries of experience-based-wisdom, have come up with certain things which desk clerks are never allowed to say when dealing with any guest. The underlying/overriding intent is to suggest to *every* guest—good or bad, rude or unbearable or both—that they will always be welcomed back, and greeted, upon arrival, with one of those great big toothy, obviously phony, leering hotel grins… and a lot of mindless blinking.

I've never been clear on whether guests actually want that or the owners of hotels only believe they do. At any rate guests of every stripe have all now grown to expect it, and when it's not delivered as soon as they set foot inside the door, the slight is carried around within them like a festering wound until they depart and, apparently, for many months after.

To sidestep further drama, we avoid saying certain things.

These then are just a few of the things that we are not ever allowed to say to any guest.

"As I JUST EXPLAINED to you…"

"I agree with you completely. It makes no sense to me either, but I don't own this joint; I just work here."

"How would you do that if you were at home?"

"How would you do that at home?" would be especially handy—and therefor is especially forbidden—because, when many guests walk through the front door of any hotel, all memory of how to accomplish the simplest, normal, everyday task is erased completely from their minds. So, we get calls, typically exasperated, often accusatory in nature, rarely civil, never apologetic, asking us how to:

Turn on a TV

Turn on a light

Turn off a light

Open a window

Lock a door

Unlock a door

Use an elevator

Operate a hair dryer, a clock radio, or an iron

These are just some of the things guests are incapable of doing unassisted.

They also demonstrate a predictable inability to:

Remember what you just told them.

Remember what you just told them again.

Remember what you just told them for the third time.

OR make sense out of the most common of common sense statements.

They do however remember how rude you were as you explained to them yet again the extraordinarily complicated process involved in using a front door key.

THE ETERNAL MYSTERY OF THE SECOND KEY

Let me ask you a question. If you check into a small hotel and they hand you a key ring with two distinctly different keys on it, and one of those keys opens the door to your room, could you guess what that other key might be for? Wait, I have that wrong.

I meant to say, if you check into a small hotel and they hand you a key ring with two distinctly different keys on it, and one of those keys opens the door to your room, would you at very least wonder, for even the briefest moment, what that other key might be for? Forget, if you will—because many of our guests seem to—that the person who handed you those keys told you clearly what that other, larger, distinctly different key is for.

Here's a follow-up question. If you, later that evening, found yourself locked out of that small hotel and your room key didn't open the front door— in fact did not even fit into the keyhole—would you then maybe start to consider, if only briefly, what that other key might be for? Would you, perhaps, try to put that larger, distinctly different key into the keyhole where your room key did not willingly go, or would you continue to try your room key and after several repeated attempts, and as many failures, lean on the doorbell seeking assistance in the demanding task of entering a building to which you have been given a key?

Tell me this:
How many times could your generous vision of human intelligence withstand the following conversation before

the wings that hold it aloft become too tattered to any longer sustain lift, and your evaluation begins to nosedive?

Typically I have just been ripped from a sound sleep by the doorbell when this conversation takes place. Yes, I know it's part of my job—but, I am RIPPED from a SOUND SLEEP by the DOORBELL, in the middle of the night.
"Yes?" I say sleepily into the intercom.
"I'm a guest here and I'd *LIKE* to get in," they snap back.
"You don't have your keys with you?"
"Yes, I have my keys."
"Then you have a key to that door."
"Which key is it?"

Because I've been ripped from a sound sleep to deal with this I am not always in a game playing mood. Otherwise, I guess I would laugh in a grandfatherly manner and say, "Well, let's see if we can work this out together. It's *not* the one you already know the use for, which does not fit into that lock. So, with that in place, let's apply the process of elimination and see if we can't begin to narrow it down."

It is amazing to me how many guests choose to ignore the possibility that the second key—the only other key on that keyring—might serve some purpose.

When this occurs during office hours—after the door is locked in the evening—I get up and go down the hallway and open the door for them. And, so that they might know in the future, I calmly say, "You have a key to this door." Then these guests always, ALWAYS, say, "The key doesn't work."

Then they demonstrate that fact by showing me that their room key refuses to go into a slot that was not designed to accept it. Then they say, "See. It doesn't fit."

Then I calmly, calmly now, say, "Let me see your keys." I take their keys and I insert the OTHER key, the mystery key, the one that, until that very moment, they apparently thought served no purpose whatsoever, into the slot *it* was designed for, and turn it. Click it goes.

"OH," they say, but never in an apologetic manner, always in the slightly dumbfounded manner of someone who has just witnessed a magic trick.

"OH!" they exclaim, "THAT's what that key is for!"

At this point I DO NOT strangle them to death one by one on the door step and drag their bodies out to the curb. I do not look them in the eye and ask them any of the various questions concerning brute intelligence which might reasonably come to mind under such circumstances. I do not mutter to myself. Instead, I say nothing. And, as I walk away I can't help thinking about what has transpired; that's why the smile I give them as they stroll by the office—still chattering about the miracle they've just witnessed—may seem to lack the profound warmth that human contact is said to generate in other people.

At night the question haunts me, pursuing me throughout the night with sharpened teeth. It's not even a complicated question like: If my brother's cousin is my father-in-law's sister's son, who am I? It's a simple question, more like, if someone gave you two keys and you knew what one of them was for, would you, if you found yourself locked out, begin to wonder about the other one?

Or, would you, as many guests do, ring the doorbell?

SOMETHING ABOUT RUDENESS

I always have hope when an arriving guest stands before me, even if they are worn out and dull-eyed from their journey. But, when my exploratory effort to raise the spark of wit within them fails, I'm always disappointed, because I expect more from my fellow humans. I know when to stop digging, of course. Basically though—all that aside—if people are nice to me, I'm nice to them in return.

However, if they are cold or superior, demanding or just completely unbearable in any of the many ways that such people have, I treat them as any reasonable person would, with ringingly cold courtesy. If they think they want to threaten me, that's OK, I'm up to it. The two things I will not put up with are discourtesy to my wife, and saying things about this establishment that are not true.

But, I am seldom rude. When I am it is because that is what's called for; in many cases it is the only language the recipient understands.

Rudeness is not a crime though. If it were, every man woman and child in New York City would be behind bars, and most of the people in New Jersey (those that aren't already). One hundred percent of the people who hold government jobs, in which they deal with people, either over the counter or over the telephone, would have to be locked up for life. Every cab driver in every nation on earth would be continually up on charges, along with every guy who drives a Porsche, a black BMW, or Land Rover (not that that would be such a loss).

And where would Macy's, Bloomingdale's, Saks Fifth Avenue and Nordstrom's find people to replace all of their incarcerated sales clerks? It must be difficult as it is finding enough people willing to work for a miserable hourly wage in exchange for the illusory right to tower over customers with chilling aristocratic condescension.

One time, a man came into the office, sat down, and began to tell me that Sylvie had been rude to him.

"Nonsense," I said, cutting him off coldly. "That woman has never been rude to anyone in her entire life. Courtesy is embedded in every fiber of her being."

While he looked at me, somewhat startled, I took the opportunity to expand on the theme. "She may have told you something you didn't want to hear, or she might not have given you the answer you would have preferred— many people seem to think that is rude—but there is no way she was rude to you."

"And how do you know that?" he asked.

"I know that, because I know the woman," I said. "But," I added, as he got up and started to walk away, "if you'd really like someone to show you what rude is, I'll be glad to do that for you."

Let's face it, if being rude to super-sensitive self-appointed aristocrats, jackasses, salesmen and other scam artists, is a crime, I was guilty long before I was hired here. And, I'll be guilty until the day I hang, resigned, pallid, long-last at peace, and completely unrepentant.

THE HANDSHAKE

One of those guys who thinks that every interaction between two males is a challenge showed up in front of my desk. It was clear from his stance and the look in his eye that he'd spent most of his life in the military and proudly, in a position of authority, and my guess would be the Marines. That I had never been through any of that, and gladly, was evident to him. He could smell it on me. Or at least that was the look of it on his face. As far as he was concerned, we were natural enemies. Life, for him was a battlefield and the act of checking in, a skirmish.

"What can I do for you?" I said in a normal manner.

"You can check us in," was his cold reply.

'Do you have a reservation?"

"If I didn't, I wouldn't be standing here."

"OK. Please, have a seat. What name is the reservation under?"

"I prefer to stand."

"As you wish. What is the name?"

"Billows."

"Ok, Mr. Billows, you're here for three nights?"

"We'll see about that."

"Well, you've reserved for three nights, you're welcome to stay three nights; please let us know if your plans change." Apparently this required no acknowledgement.

"I'll need a credit card to pre-authorize," I say.

"I gave you my credit card number when I reserved the room."

"Yes, but we'd like to run the card—pre-authorize an amount that will cover your stay."

He painfully and unwillingly removes his wallet, fishes around in it for a credit card. As I reach to accept the card, instead of placing it in my hand, he flips it casually onto the desk. Because I'm 62 years old and have already had enough of that kind of nonsense in my life, I simply pick the thing up and run it through the machine, just as though I had no desire to stand up and hit him as hard as I possibly could right in the nose. And, since this is Life and not some kind of wonderful dream, the credit card doesn't work. It comes back DECLINED.

"Do you have another card we might use perhaps; this one has been declined."
The very good and delightful Mr. Billows snatches the card from my hand. He fishes out another card and tosses it beyond my still outstretched hand onto the desk. At this point, not being one of those who truly believes that it is part of the job to put up with every bastard that enters our front door, I give the guy a look. He looks back at me coldly. There is a little bit of challenge in it. I would love to stand up and just level the son-of-a-bitch but I'm wearing a hand-painted tie from Venice, and I understand that it's difficult to get blood out of silk... that, and the fact that I've never hit another human being in my life. But, the impulse is certainly there.

Once that's all aside I hand him the keys and tell him the room number and instruct him as to the use of the front door key and offer to help him with his luggage if he should so desire. But, Mr. Billows does not so desire.
"OK. You're in room 508; would you like me to show you to 508?"

"I'll find it without your help."

Ten minutes later, Billows is calling down to ask for a couple of extra pillows and a couple of glasses.

I say, "There are extra pillows in the closet or in one of the drawers, and the glasses are on the bathroom counter."

"Nope," he says, "Neither. I've looked."

"I'll be glad to bring you some glasses and an extra pillow or two," I say.

"We need three," he says.

"Or, three," I say.

"Make it three," he warns, "I'll expect three."

Before I can race downstairs to gather up pillows for this fine gentleman, the phone rings.

While I'm on the phone a man appears before me with a clipboard; he wants me to sign for a package. The phone rings again and while I'm on that line, the chef calls on another line; he has a change in the menu. Before I can complete that, two couples arrive simultaneously both wishing to check in. The womanly half of the first couple has 43,000 questions and, after she's comfortably seated, she asks them very slowly, very casually; she has all the time in the world; she's on vacation and feeling kinda chatty. When I ask if they would like me to show them to their room, naturally she says yes. During the elevator ride up, she has come up with more questions, so, when we arrive at their room, I'm pinned there, nodding and smiling and doing the best I can to suggest to her, subtly, that I have a greater destiny, something beyond standing throughout eternity in her doorway fielding her every flighty concern.

While checking in the second couple, Mr. Billows calls down again. He sounds gruff. "Where are those pillows?" I say, "I'll bring them right up." While the second couple waits for the elevator, I race downstairs to gather up pillows and I am stopped in the hall by a guest who wants to know where the ice is. "Are there any buckets?" I head to the elevator, which is now on another floor and push the button. I find myself facing yet another couple with bags. They wish to check in. I go to the office with the pillows, put them aside, and check in all the waiting guests as they arrive in small herds and accumulate in the hallway. Seeing the pillows, suddenly they all want extra pillows as well.

When I look up, there is an old lady standing before me with 32,000 questions. She looks remarkably like the one who asked the 43,000 questions earlier, and, like her, she takes her time in asking them. As always, each answer seems to generate yet another batch of questions. I give her 32,000 pleasant answers—some long, some short, some with maps, some with witticisms thrown in. I don't dawdle but I'm courteous. It's a tightrope. It's my job. I like to pretend that I believe that I'm good at it.
I'm not entirely convinced.

The phone rings and I take a reservation. Then, I notice the message waiting light is lit and ignore it. Someone wants me to show them where the steps are; someone else wants me to recommend a good place, within a one block radius, which serves the best Lithuanian food in America. The chef calls again with another change to the menu; it seems that we'll be having the lobster bisque after all. Four couples now arrive simultaneously and the maids tell me the dryer is not working. The maids appear one by one before me and dump the doorknobs to various closets, bathrooms and entry doors which have come off in their hands. I have no time for any of this. My greatest desire on earth at that moment is to get those pillows to Mr. Billows.

The owner comes in looking for the keys to his office. I go to retrieve the ones which I have personally marked "RETURN THESE KEYS HERE IMMEDIATELY AFTER USE" but they're not there.
Mr. Billows calls down again asking, "Do you INTEND to bring us pillows?"
"Mr. Billows," I sigh, "I am living proof of the fact that a man can only be in 37 places at once." He doesn't get it; he doesn't like it; maybe both…maybe neither. It doesn't matter.
He says, "It's not asking too much to get a couple extra pillows is it?" and slams the phone down.
"A FEW," I say to the dead receiver, "you asked for a few."

I pick up the pillows and the phone rings. Someone wants to know how to call down to the front desk. I'm stunned for a moment. I say, "This is the front desk; you've reached the front desk."
They say, "Yes, but I couldn't reach you before."
I have no idea what they are talking about and so I say, "I have no idea what you are talking about." It seemed like a reasonable thing to say. They explain that there are these buttons along the top of the phone which—in theory—you can push and reach: the front desk, the restaurant, the wake-up service, the current time. At this hotel none of these

buttons work. So, now I know what the person is talking about.

"Dial O," I say, "Forget the buttons," I say. "Just dial O."

"I had to call you on my cell phone!" he complains. "Those buttons should work," he continues. "Why don't they work? Why have them at all if they don't work?"

This is a fair question which might also be applied to cell phones. My grandmother's phone worked better than the best cell phone you can purchase today, and it had a dial with 10 numbers on it, nothing more; had better sound too. Still, the guest had a point which I both understood and agreed with entirely.

"I understand," I say. "I am in complete agreement with you," I say. "If it was up to me, they would work."

"Well, why don't you fix the damned phone so that it works?" he shouts.

"Well, first," I say, "as I said, I'm in complete agreement with you. But, second, unfortunately, I have nothing to do with it."

"Who does?"

"The owner."

"The owner fixes phones?"

Actually the owner expressly forbids others to fix the phones, but I can't say that, so I say, "No, but the owner is the man you have to talk to about those buttons."

"That's absurd! That is absurd!"

"Again, I could not agree with you more. But, again, it's not up to me."

"Well, you are just delighted to do nothing about this aren't you?"

Actually, I hate being unable to do anything about that; it irritates me every moment of my existence here. But, I can't explain that because my accuser has hung up.

Here we have a little bit of a philosophical schism. The owner believes that when a person pushes a button marked, let's say FRONT DESK, an acceptable result is no result whatsoever. I think—and this is where my wacky side reveals itself—I think that when a guest pushes a button that is marked FRONT DESK something should happen. And to further reveal my insanity, I think what should happen is this: they should reach the front desk.

Once that's cleared up, I dash out the door and lock it and, since the elevator is, as Fate would have it, somewhere on some other floor, I dash UP the five flights of stairs taking pillows to Billows. I am chanting, "Taking pillows to Billows" to myself, and finding myself unreasonably entertained by the little rhyme as I arrive at the gentleman's door all a-sweat, a'grinnin' an' bearin' pillows.
He answers my knock, takes the pillows and says, "I asked for three."
"We have a full house; two is all I can offer you at the moment. I'll look around though."
"What about the glasses?" he snaps.
"Glasses?"
"I asked for glasses."
OH! I had completely forgotten about the glasses. I grin apologetically. "There should be glasses on the bathroom counter," I say weakly.
"There aren't," he says.

"Are you sure?" I say, and regret it even as the words leave my lips.

Of course, getting a couple of glasses to Mr. Billows is a snap. They appear as if by magic in my upturned palms and, while he's still standing there, I simply hand them over. He smiles, calls me Buddy, chucks me under the chin and offers me the hand of his youngest daughter in marriage. Doves flutter about, the ceiling opens above and there is nothing but blue skies as far as the weary eye can see. Unfortunately, I'm already married and unfortunately it didn't happen that way. But, it did happen. I mean I did manage, some twenty minutes later, to hand two glasses through the door to a frowning and silent Mr. Billows, but not before he called down and left another message, while I was plunging the toilet in the room next to his.

Later that evening, my wife and I are in the office together when this guy, Billows and his perfectly reasonable, perfectly attractive, quiet little wife are passing by. He stops, he enters, he stands before us. I stand up.

He smiles and says, in a folksy, aw-shucks sort of way, "You know, there *were* extra pillows in the drawer, under the TV. We would have never thought to look there. And, after you brought the glasses, my wife found a couple in the bathroom." He steps forward. He offers me his hand.

I   do   not   take   it.

Mr. Billows is standing there in front of his good wife with his hand extended, and I am standing there in front of my good wife looking the man in the eye. I do not move. He's fixed in place, hand extended.

I make no move whatsoever.

He doesn't know what to make of my behavior.
I know exactly what I'm doing.

My guess is that, until that very moment Mr. Billows had gone through life offending people, talking down to them and just generally treating them badly, being an entrenched bastard at every available opportunity, knowing that later he would make it all better simply by shaking hands with his victims. Then, of course, all would be forgiven.

Mr. Billows thinks that my position here, as a slave to this establishment, demands that I shake his hand. I think that I've already done enough for this stupid prick. So, I stand riveted, unmoving, looking that man right straight in the eye, until he goes away.

After they are gone, my wife informs me that this is improper hospitality industry behavior.

GUESTS ARE PEOPLE TOO

P. D. Ouspensky, in his efforts to first discover, then disentangle, and ultimately define the fundamental metaphysical nature of man, cast about briefly before suggesting that we must begin by first admitting that we know nothing. Unfortunately however, that's not true. We do know something. What we know is that some people are, as my very dear wife puts it, absolutely unbearable.

Whether you are in the hotel business or not, that is the Alpha and the Omega of our fundamental metaphysical reality; some people are absolutely unbearable. Even the briefest contact with some guests would dis-settle, disturb and dishearten the Buddha. Some people are absolutely unbearable. In the hotel business we, frail, earth-bound, mere mortals with no pure universal archetypal wisdom upon which to draw, have this point driven home with a kind of nagging, seemingly never-ending, viciousness a dozen times each day. I exaggerate of course, it's probably no more than eleven times a day, and I know it will end someday, when we rest at last in our grave.

To complicate things just a little hotel owners insist that, when dealing with the endless complaints of someone who is absolutely unbearable, we must keep in mind the fact that their problems are all somehow *our* fault. The owner's view is that if we handle an absolutely unbearable guest properly we can coax them into extending their stay, thus prolonging the pleasure of their smoldering presence, or possibly persuade them into promising to return, so that we might experience that joy on a more regular basis.

The unbearable aspect of some guests aside, I think I can get closer to the truth. Years of experience in the hotel business has provided me percentages. With great pleasure I can tell you, and quite sincerely that almost 90% of the people who walk through our door are the salt-of-the-earth, and they are good, if not excellent, guests.

For a small taste of that let me relate how one evening two women showed up in front of the office with a question. I was on the phone at the moment taking a reservation and the owner's wife, Madame, interrupted her check writing to cheerfully ask in personable, lovely, bell-like tones, "How may I help you?"

One of the women stepped into the office and asked where she could find some ice, and Madame, who will never again win any hearing contests… and, in fairness, whose first language is not English, said this: "Thank you; that is very kind of you to say so. But it was not always so nice, it took a lot of work and many many years, and we are not done yet I am afraid."
The woman, not completely undaunted, said, "ICE."
Madame said, "Thank you again. There is much more to do, of course. But, that is very kind of you to notice, Madame, and kind of you to say."
"Well, you've certainly done a very nice job," said the woman in a cheerful tone and looked around with exaggerated admiration.
(May God bless that good woman ten thousand ways.)

Then she went out into the hallway and whispered something to her friend as they began to walk away.

By that time I was wrapping up the reservation and I got up and quickly went after them. I told them that the ice machine could be found downstairs. These ladies, these good guests, these wonderful people, thanked me quietly. "She doesn't hear very well, does she?" one asked in a whisper, as if Madame might somehow hear that.
"No, but she is absolutely delightful," I said, somewhat proudly.
"Oh, she certainly is," they both agreed.

Then came the questions for which Madame has already begun to supply some of the answers: How long have they owned the hotel? Where did they come from in France? Were they hoteliers in France? The compliments which Madame thought she had received earlier soon followed. "The entire place is just lovely! And the restaurant is excellent. Very nice. We just love it here."

THROUGH THE GRILLE

At this small privately owned French hotel there is no wall separating the office and the lobby, there is only an iron grille; one of the owner's earliest and most misunderstood aesthetic decisions. I say misunderstood because those of us who don't like the thing probably lack the aesthetic sophistication to fully appreciate any egregious eyesore.

What's peculiar is that our guests don't seem to understand that we see everything that is done, and hear everything that is said, in that lobby, through that grille. They can see us, but somehow feel that we can not see them. They can hear us, but assume that, by some quirk in the laws of audio physics, we can't hear them.

One of the first things that is said when they enter, is how hot or how stuffy or how warm or how unbearable it is in this building. It is a simple fact, universally recognized, but there is nothing to be done about it. And although I am in complete agreement with them, I get tired of hearing it.

There is nothing more to be said on this matter, so, we pout a little, we shrug, and we move on. Or, in my case, we harp about it endlessly and loudly, pacing and snarling and snapping and occasionally throwing things, refusing to back off and refusing to move on.
"We LIVE in the TWENTY-FIRST century for God's sake!" we growl…and we do not move on. Most people who work here, however, have moved on long ago. But most people are free to leave this God forsaken place and seek fresh air once in a while.

(I have the feeling that when this sees print I'll be free to leave this place and seek as much fresh air as I might wish.)

After dining in the restaurant, while sitting around in the lobby moaning about how *stuffed* they are and picking their teeth, our native customers scream at each other in shrill voices. It is easy to see why the French may think that we Americans are loud, crude and tasteless. After listening to them through the grille, it would be difficult to draw any other conclusion. If the good folks assembled in our lobby are a good example of what we have to offer, we are not only loud, crude, and tasteless, we are also extraordinarily proud of our stupidity.

When we say something which demonstrates our lack of even the most basic education, we employ the full force of our lungs; when we say something that shows our adamant refusal to accept anyone who doesn't look like, think like, and act like the guy we see in the mirror each morning, we proclaim it like writ.
Why I should be embarrassed by this, I do not know.

Volume, vulgarity, vacuity, vapidity and vileness aside, the thing that disturbs me most is the misinformation that passes between my generally jovial (drunk), small-minded, well-intentioned, loud-mouthed fellow Americans, in that tiny, airless, tapestry-laden room. Much of it has to do with the history of this establishment. For reasons which I am completely unable to explain, I find these contrivances even more irritating than the volume at which they are delivered. Or, it just occurs to me now, maybe I'm just jealous; maybe I'd like to join in and do a little boisterous lying of my own… put my skills to the test. Frequently I'm tempted to intervene, make corrections, but I know that would be wrong. I know that it would be wrong, for example, to shout through the grille, "You don't know what the hell you're talking about!" So, I remain as mute as a carp. It might even be wrong for me to mumble quietly to myself, "What utter nonsense!", and sometimes I don't do that either.

Here are some of the things I've overheard concerning the restaurant, none of which are true: It used to be a speakeasy. It used to be an Irish pub. It used to be a jazz club. It used to be an private club for retired circus performers. Someone once cultivated mushrooms down there. Until 1972 (the year of the big raid, apparently) they grew marijuana down there (you can still see where all the indoor/outdoor lighting was attached to the ceiling). The place is haunted by a ghost imported from France by way of one of the many life-sized statues which reside there among the tables and tapestries. (Actually, that one I admired.) That it was once an indoor salt water pool I find less impressive as lies go, but it'd be cool.

Here are some of the things I've overheard concerning the hotel, none of which are true:
It used to be owned by an Italian (Greek, Spanish, Irish, English, Swedish, anything but French) family. It used to be a private residence (though why a private residence would be divided into 50 small rooms each with its own bath is never explained). It used to be the largest nautical library in the United States of America (six full floors of books on boats). It was once owned by a large foreign-

based (usually Japanese) corporation and each floor was divided into two huge suites where top level executives resided and spent most of their free time sitting around in leather wing-back chairs smoking cigars and sipping cognac while smiling smugly under wizened brows and clinging to the bare legs of scantily clad young blonde women, each much younger than themselves, their wives or their own (fully clothed, dark haired) daughters. That all came to an end, of course, one black Friday. That it had burned to the ground in the late 1940's and was rebuilt to resemble the original 1910 structure. The restoration apparently included the wear and tear on all the woodwork, the clunking, clanking, banging, ever-uncooperative, original-style, steam heating system, the screeching plumbing, the somewhat questionable electricity, the creaking floorboards, the multi-layer painted moldings, and convincing replicas of the original cast iron, ball and claw-foot tubs. That there is a miniature golf course on the roof is not true, but that would be cool too.

I've also heard, through that grille, that the owner killed a man in Paris—or rather, beat him to within an inch of his life—and fled to the United States to avoid justice. This one seems especially popular. I've heard it more than once, from more than one customer... through that grille. Apparently, the owner stopped by to pick up his devoted wife and his darling young daughter as he fled. Nothing speeds up a hasty departure like a woman and a kid.

The staff in the office at this small hotel also overhears—such is our blessing—every cell phone conversation that takes place in that room, and they are all, each and every one of them, VERY important. The greatest business decisions ever made in the history of the western economic system were made very loudly in that very room over cell phones. We also hear how much every loving mommy loves and misses her little darlings (vewy-wery-wery much) and how soon mommy and daddy will be home (before you know it). Then we hear how much they love them and miss them again, and perhaps, if we're lucky, something will call us away from the desk so we won't have to hear it a third time. We hear some lullabies sung sweetly. We hear some folk tunes too—most frequently "You Are My Sunshine" and most frequently sung off key, but it's a hard tune to carry. And, as said, we also hear every casual conversation that takes place between guests.

During the wee-wah convention we might, through the grille, learn by osmosis a little something about wee-wahs; during the food convention we might find out something we really didn't want to know about pre-prepared food; during the lab technicians' convention we might learn something we hope our dear wife had not also overheard… lest, by strange coincidence, she come down with it herself within a week.

When the Apple Convention convenes in January each year, we are full to overflowing with apostles vociferously proselytizing for their truly remarkable, unsurpassed and unsurpassable, lovable and much beloved computer system. Although I have never had anyone try to sell me on the benefits, wonders, and glories of the PC, I have never met a single Apple user under any circumstance who did not feel compelled to take the opportunity to at least try to put me on the right path. This peculiar, perhaps slightly abnormal commitment to a product is both foreign and astounding to me—I'm just not a nylon jacket and matching baseball cap kind of guy—but that is not to say these folks are not good people. They are very good guests as well, coming and going with delight in their elfin eyes, anxious to share the most recent miracles of the Apple world mostly with each other, but with the great unwashed and uninformed as well; always leaving early to the convention center and returning late, loaded down with the latest tiny, shiny, plastic-encased digital distraction. It is a harmless little cult.

They are clean and quiet and demand almost nothing; they are hearty eaters and joyous of nature and an abnormal percentage of them look and move and dress like one of the seven dwarves (a startling number like Doc). All that aside, they are excellent guests, and we're always glad to see them. We blush appropriately when they wag their fingers at us because our office is still run on PCs.

They are surpassed by the geologists, who come in December, filling the place with an unusual calm. I like these good people particularly because they not only allow me to answer a direct question with a direct answer, they prefer it. I have taken several of these people quietly aside at one time or another and asked them each the same question. "Are things as bad geologically as some people say they are?" And, each of them has told me this, "They're worse, but we can't get anybody to listen to us." I usually say, "It seems like a lot of people *are* listening to you." And they reply, "I wish that were true. Even those who are listening have no idea how bad it is."

As guests the geologist are only surpassed by the Japanese. The geologist I told this to said he was sure he spoke for all of our geological guests in saying what a great honor it was to be so recognized. I agreed that second place was better than not having placed at all.

As to the Japanese, they are everything a good hotel guest should, or even could be; clean, quiet, unassuming, undemanding, extraordinarily (almost painfully) courteous, generous to the maids and servers and a pleasure to deal with on every level. Their weird way of warping simple English language phrases into surprising, even startlingly new constructs demonstrates conclusively that genius is occasionally invested in ignorance. Based primarily on the free exchange of R's and L's their use of our language is at times confusing, but always entertaining. To hear a Japanese gentleman ask, Whele is the nealest *coll-lentar?*, is a joy…a puzzling kind of joy, but a joy nonetheless.

During the chemists' convention two chemical guys were sitting in the lobby and I happened to overhear their conversation. It went something like this:
"And how do you activate the incipient plasmafication of a stagnant di-chlora-bi-hexidrate?" asked the first.
"Well," said the other casually, "We just add a solution of short-variant theta-thoodimate with ferrous pillium!"
They both laughed hysterically at this. From all indications this was the funniest thing any chemist had ever said. They were both in there slapping their thighs and rolling around on the couch, until one of them regained enough composure to choke out, "Or…" he sputtered, "Or…you could simply

heat it to minus 37 degrees and introduce a boreal suspension!"
Neither of these guys was capable of recovering his breath after that one. They were both bent in two, gasping for air. "Oh, man," one of them finally wheezed, "I know a guy who actually tried that." This thought tied them up in knots again. I had no idea there was such humor in chemistry or that chemists were such clowns.

When old folks gather, talk turns with alacrity to surgery, pills, and death. It's always casual, always matter of fact, with an occasional "Oh my!" thrown in.
"Did you know Will Turnbull died?"
"No. My goodness. When did that happen?"
"Last Friday night. Kidney failure."
"Oh my...You know, to be perfectly honest with you, I thought he was already dead..."
"You know, I did too. For some reason I thought it was right around the time of Ada's hip replacement... but apparently not."
"What happened?"
"She was always so frail I thought for sure she would go first...Well... anyway, he looked a little yellow at dinner; she told him to sit up straight and stop slurping his soup. After dessert he didn't look any better; she took him right to the emergency room."
"He was always such a generous tipper."
"Yes, yes he was. No winsome waitress ever went hungry after waiting on Will. And that man could whistle!"
"Really? You know I never heard him whistle."
"Oh yes. He whistled just like a bird."

"Huh…You know, I really thought that he died sometime early last year."

"Yes, I thought so too. But, that's why it came as such a shock. I was sure he'd gone already."

"It was in the Spring wasn't it?"

"Yes, as I recall it *was* around that time. I thought, 'Poor Will.' Well, none of us last forever, I guess."

"Well, no, apparently not. Anyway, in the emergency room…you know how they always make you wait… After waiting an hour or two, they told her it was not an emergency, and she should take him home, and they should go in to talk to their regular doctor on Monday. Of course by that time he was gone."

"My goodness. I don't know how many times I've heard that same story."

"Yes, it's such a shame. But, say, have they ever placed you on Veloproxin?"

"Oh my goodness yes. I took chloro-bi-hex-a-drine for years but they decide to switch me to Veloproxin when it came out, and I must say I felt so much better. For a while, in the beginning. But now they got this…Oh what is it…Hollo-de-exilate or something. They say it's better for your liver."

"That's what they claim yes, but I don't believe it."

"I hope they put me on that. I'd like to give it a try; it's new. All the girls down at the clubhouse are on it and they're all just so pleased with themselves."

"I'll have to ask my doctor about it. How about Doro-flatilate? Have they ever had you on that?

One evening quite late, there's an ancient, tiny woman sitting in the lobby alone, reading. Her daughter has abandoned her there. She's been sitting in the same chair, working her way slowly through a nice thick book for hours when I speak through the screen.
"What are you reading?"

There's some confusion at first because she can hear me but she doesn't see anyone else in the lobby. So, it's a delight and something of a relief when she turns to discover that I'm behind her, looking over her shoulder, through the grille. She shows me the cover of the book. It looks like it's about 800 pages and she's very near the end—she has maybe 30 pages to go.
I say, "That's a pretty impressive book. What's it about?"
"Oh it's about Semitism," she says. "I don't know if it's for it or against it, I haven't figured that out yet."
I laugh heartily.
"I sure hope I find out soon," she says, and smiles at me nicely through the grille.

That's the beginning of a pleasant conversation, and by the time her daughter returns, we've taken a genuine liking to each other.

She was wonderful.

GOOD PEOPLE, NOT ALWAYS GOOD GUESTS

Most guests come and go leaving little impression one way or the other of their presence, their absence, their departure, their return; and an amazing number of them seem to be yanked from a strictly limited number of common molds. By that I mean, whenever I look up and there is a white, middle-aged, married couple standing before me like Tweedle-dum and Tweedle-dee, and I ask, "Yes, how may I help you?" it always throws me when they say, "We'd like to check in."
I could honestly swear in a court of law that we already have them here, or, if not, we already have something close enough. Still, that throws me every time...that, and their inability to find a bathroom.

Place these salt-of-the-earth guests in a room with three doors and they are completely lost. When I show them to their room, immediately after entering that room, one of them—usually the male—will go directly to the closet, open it up and declare contentiously, "This is not the bathroom!" OR, maybe, "This is a closet!" They follow that observation immediately with a somewhat frantic question, "Where is the bathroom?" OR a somewhat huffy accusation, "We were TOLD this room had a private bath."

At this point I am always at a slight disadvantage because I am tempted to speak my mind, which, of course, I do not. That would be wrong. In any business setting it is always forbidden to confront idiocy head on, no matter how pure the idiocy and no matter how perfect the set-up. Showing guests to their room is not a vaudeville act, and our guests

are not here to play straight man for some of the most
obvious quips on earth.

I'm sure you understand already, but here's the scene:
We've just walked into a room with three doors. One of
them, we've just passed through. One of them, as the guest
has noticed, is not the bathroom. If things are going
normally, the door we've just come in through is still open,
and if we look out there we can see that, for some reason,
one of the two guests is still standing out there in the hall,
blinking at us. Give her a little wave, and she waves back.

So, with two doors eliminated... I say nothing. I bite my
heavily shredded tongue and I say nothing. I make no
comment whatsoever. In silence I step over to the last
remaining door, open it, reach one hand in and flip on the
light. The guest then, always, ALWAYS, (always, for
God's sake) ALWAYS goes through that door to check it
out for himself. Despite the enormous odds that I might be
right, he looks in. He wants to be sure that I am not pulling
a fast one on him, running a scam of some sort, only
pretending that it's the door to the bathroom. This occurs
with (I'm sorry to say) 85% of the people who check in
here for the first time. Let me add quickly (again), these are
good people and good guests, and I welcome them. These
good people are, by comparison (as you will see), a joy.
And, I'm sure there must be humor in this three door skit
for some, but for me, it has lost its charm.

Good guests would make *excellent* guests if they were
capable of doing the simplest thing without assistance—
turn on a light switch, plug in a TV which the maids have

in their cleaning frenzy managed to unplug, put a key into a lock, turn a key once it is in the lock, open a window or close a window, or discover the extra blankets which are on the closet shelf in plain sight, precisely where I told them they would be.

I believe strongly in these people, and want to believe that they could do all of these things by themselves, but they can't or won't, and usually don't. They are incapable. Or, they are unwilling. It makes me wonder how they manage to survive out there in the real world. When they call down to the front desk to ask, How do I reach the front desk? I find myself at a complete loss.

After many years of this, it just gets so very tiresome.

Anyone might become peevish...most, I suppose, would hide it better, of course. But, please hear my cry. When a guest calls down asking how to accomplish the most normal, everyday task, I am forbidden to say, "Well, think about it. How would you do that if you were at home?" Instead I go up and show them how a shower works or how to dial 'O', or how to close the curtains. I open the drawer to show them the extra pillows that I told them were in that drawer. See. Here's the drawer. With each hand you take one of these drawer pulls between thumb and forefinger. Now tug on them gently in an outward direction. Now, look inside...Oh, my goodness, there they are! While I'm here, let me show you how to remove a pillow from a drawer. As for using the pillow... just put it over my face and press down firmly until I stop struggling.

Suddenly, I find myself facing a man who is maybe forty-six or forty-eight years old. He is nicely dressed. He has a wife with him and she's nicely attired. They are a respectable couple. They appear to be intelligent, well-educated people. They own a home in Santa Barbara and they've put three completely self-centered, self-serving, arrogant offspring through Stanford. In short: they've done OK. I guess the gentleman is upper echelon management in some huge multi-national corporation and hauls down six figures. But, unfortunately, he can't make it around the block without assistance.

Parking is across the street, and to get to us they've already passed it by. To get back there, he'll have to go around the block. He's actually asked me to draw him a map showing how to do that. This is the second time I've explained to the man that the street upon which he has most recently driven is one-way. He hadn't really noticed that.

"When you step outside our door," I say, without the slightest trace of exasperation, "*look* across the street and you can *see* the garage. To get there however, since this is a one-way street, you must go around the block." At this point I scribe a large square with my finger in the air. "I suggest you take a series of right hand turns."

This statement—take a series of rights—challenges the good man's navigational skills, stretching them beyond their limit. The dull look on his face makes it difficult for me to keep my seat. I don't know what keeps me from going around to his side of the desk, grabbing him by the shoulders and shaking him while yelling loudly into his ear- WAKE UP!

What world do these people dwell in? That a reasonably successful, well educated, supposedly intelligent and undoubtedly nice, upper-middle-class American male is incapable of understanding the fundamental geometric surety that underlies four consecutive right hand turns makes me absolutely one hundred percent insane. Yet, I do not show it…well, I try very hard not to. Surely in his many years here on this planet this man has made use of that tactic before. Go around the goddamned block; it's not a new concept. That any human being can *look at* the garage across the street and yet be incapable of getting there by car…is impossible for me to believe. Ask any five year-old what the result might be if he took four right hand turns and he will tell you. Birds, with brains the size of a split pea, have the ability to navigate from Canada to the Antarctic and back without instruction of any sort.

I will never be convinced that the human race is not still divided between Neanderthal and Cro-Magnon. Additionally, I find myself continually amazed at how well the Neanderthals seem to do financially.

At times, depending upon my mood I'm guessing, and whether I have time for such idiocy, I will go out onto the sidewalk with the gentleman and point to the parking lot across the street. "It's that one that looks like a parking lot," I explain. I point at the corner where they are to make their first turn, and, again, I make an exaggerated motion in the air which even a turtle would understand to mean go around the damned block.

Sometimes this helps.

It really does seem that far too many of us are nothing more than lumbering louts. I suppose that sounds judgmental. On the other hand, I'm sure that those of you who must deal with people on a daily basis will think I'm being far too generous in that assessment. But, to look across the counter into the empty eyes of some dullard, knowing that any attempt to enkindle the residual spark of long-lost wit would be wasted effort, becomes trying after a dozen years or so. I no longer have trouble with those who display a total lack of humor—though I get my fair share of that—that, I can somehow handle. The dead fish countenance, however, always throws me.

When a human being, walking upright on two legs, comes to me and asks, "How do you get downstairs?" it makes me peevish. It's not the same as when the elevator is broken and I spend the entire day and night hauling people's luggage up and down the steps and no one in the entire crowd either thanks me or considers giving me a tip—that's different—but it makes me peevish nonetheless.

The stairs going down to the restaurant are directly next to the elevator, they are not hidden in any way, they are in plain sight; they look like stairs. And, whether you have just come down those very same stairs from your room, or have taken the elevator down, the answer is the same: to get downstairs you go down those stairs. The process is embedded in the phrase *go down stairs*. Such questions are very difficult for a guy like me to handle because of my exponentially growing distaste for stupid-iocy.

But, I've wandered.

Something like 5% of our guests are clearly distinct individuals with unique personalities, wit, charm, that sort of thing. They are good natured, reasonably intelligent, and they make very good guests; by that I mean they manage to get along pretty well without us. They want a nice, clean, comfortable and safe room in which to pass the night, and, merely by coincidence, that is precisely what we provide. They arrive happy, and when they depart they always have something nice to say. They don't spend a lot of time asking a lot of stupid questions; they go out and do stuff on their own, and when they get back, most of them don't feel the urge to stop in and tell us what they did during every minute of their excursion. They are nice to the maids, pleasant to the restaurant staff, generous to both, and just plain glad to be here. This last aspect makes us, in turn, always glad to have them here. (Thank you, 5%.)

These guests believe, as I do, that courtesy, a general congeniality, and kindness (given the chance to offer it) are essential tools for keeping this world from plummeting into ego-centric uselessness, or reverting to brute tribalism or, most likely and most regrettably, a peculiar blend of both. That's probably where we're headed anyway, but not because of anything I might say or do to a guest.

Another 4% are those rare individuals who seem exceptionally likeable; much more well-educated, witty, charming, informed, and good natured than I am or ever will be, or, for that matter, would ever care to be. They harbor a keen intelligence which is immediately evident and truly enviable; a majority of them, it would seem, are naturally gregarious.

If they become regular guests, we sometimes sit in the office late at night, when the owner's not around, and share a bottle of wine. This number, honestly, now that I think about it, is more like 3%... wait... maybe 2. And, God bless each and every one of you. There's a great deal of comfort in just knowing that you're out there. I'm pleased to say I can match your faces with your names; and, you've really made my selfless sacrifice upon the altar of this hotel, for some brief moments, bearable if not actually worthwhile.

THE FINAL PERCENT

The final 1% (if that's what it comes to) is divided amongst the demanding, the dilettante criminals, and the just plain undeniably insane. This 1% (if that is what it comes to) is the inspiration for this work. My very dear wife adds two additional types which she calls: rude and unbearable. But, to my way of thinking these are sub-sets which might be found under any of the basic types listed above, except the good guests of course; good guests are never either rude or unbearable, and helpless guests are rarely rude.

Demanding people who would not be content under any circumstances whatsoever dominate the field. It saddens me to report that many of these people are smart looking women who seem to have taken assertiveness training classes, and have taken them, apparently, very seriously. They will argue with you for an hour and a half over seven cents and, for them, it is a matter of something bigger and more important than pride. There are some of us who might, depending upon our mood at the time, undertake the grueling task of trying to free them of such a foolish idea, and thus contribute, in some small way to the advancement of civilization. Whenever I find myself facing someone who would throw their own grandmother down a flight of steps in order to save 30 cents I find it difficult to ignore the calling, and I surrender when I must, with regret.

Of course, in this noble battle over a nickel, these glaring, snappish aristocrats represent all oppressed women everywhere and so, they can not back down, and, once embroiled in the haggling, dignity no longer means anything to them, if ever it did. If screaming is required, they'll do that. If lies and unfair accusations are called for, they'll be there fully-armed. This is always painful, but worse, it is an embarrassment, not just for me, not just for women, but for all of humanity.

When I sit across from such people I sometimes try to imagine that somewhere there are little children who brighten at the sight of their arrival, and cry, GRAN-MA!, with great delight. GRAN-MA, they squeal, and go running into their open arms. This is perhaps the most difficult task I have ever asked my mind to undertake.
"Did you know that your Gran-ma turns into a snapping, snarling, vicious old shrew whenever she has to pry open her purse to pay any charge no matter how insignificant?"

From the first minute these pit bulls of micro-monetary justice call the hotel—with a thousand wary questions—until the very minute they depart—and many times, long after that—they remain solidly, unflinchingly what they are, and what they are is absolutely unbearable. By the third or fourth change in their arrival date we know, we are no longer guessing for it is a certainty, that they are either going to cancel, or much worse, they are going to show up. We wring our hands in earnest prayer for that cancellation. When they arrive, it is immediately clear from the look on their faces that they belong in a better place. But, we are forbidden to assist them in any outward direction; we cannot, for example, say, "Let me help you find a place more to your liking—*that* would be more to our liking as well." Or, "Please, let me show you how you might use our front door also as an exit."

I don't think such people would learn anything from the exercise, but it would be therapy for us; perhaps not as effective as giving them a boot in the rump on their way out, but helpful. This is a dream of course.

And perhaps no further evidence is required to prove just how unsuited I am to be in the business in which I find myself inextricably entangled.

When one of our assertiveness training graduates checks out, she has a long list of things she has found unacceptable during her stay. The things that have her so upset are: the weather, which was not to her liking for the entire time she was here (we normally ask for one week's advance notice to supply our guests with appropriate weather, and we ask that our guests try to understand that occasionally there are conflicts concerning the various types of weather our various guests might request on any given day), she also suffered through; a burned out light bulb, a noise one night which she thinks might have come from another room, a window which, once opened, let in too much air, a hand towel which had unseemly loosened threads, the cable car bell was too loud, and—just so you know, not a complaint, just an observation—they run far too frequently; a picture on the wall was slightly askew, the smell of food came seeping into her room one afternoon—something fried she thought—the walls were a color she found particularly *not* to her liking and, AND... a hair was found on the carpet in a corner of the room where the light does not reach and where no one not on their hands and knees would ever find themselves, let alone with a magnifying glass, a flashlight, a pair of tweezers, a digital camera and a plastic bag.

One wonders, of course, why, if things were so horrible, she stayed ten days. One also wonders why she didn't simply point out to us these monumentally egregious matters—those which we could do anything about—so that we might have corrected them. And, of course, later on, in our lucky future, one will wonder why she keeps coming back again and again and again. At this juncture however she demands a discount and, it saddens me deeply, it tears my very heart out, to say that, at this small privately owned French hotel, she gets it.

When we run her phone bill, of course there is say, $1.50 or more typically 50 cents, and she bristles. She is outraged; she has NEVER been the victim of such out and out cold blooded, blatant and utterly shameless robbery in her entire life. At this point she is transformed from Lillian Gish to lioness protecting her cubs. Yes, Lady, that's how we grew rich by screwing our trusting guests 50 cents at a time.

Here's a comparatively illuminating tale. My wife and I went to the mountains to ski. She made a short call to her mother who lives in the same area code (so, it was a local call). She wanted to let the good woman know that we had arrived safely. That conversation (if two sentences is a conversation) lasted less than a minute. When we checked out, that single call was $27. We paid. We winced, as anyone would, but we didn't whimper; we didn't rant or rave; we didn't sputter and threaten legal action; we didn't demand to see the manager, we didn't make a scene, we paid. One time we went to that vast emptiness to the south called L.A. to see one of the great singers sing one of the great operas. When we arrived my dear wife called her mother again and spoke with her for a very short time. Cost $46. We paid. We did not accuse the thieves of being what they were. They knew what they were and were proud of it. We didn't like it, but we paid.

In the hotel business, if a guest absolutely refuses to be pleased, that, in the owner's view, is our fault. WE must find some path by which to wheedle our way into the heart (if we can find it) and mind (which is the frightening part) of this person and…and, then what? Do a little dance I suppose. Here we have a philosophical difference… a schism in the gospel that guides hotel operations everywhere. Hotel owners always want their staff to coddle the guest who can not be satisfied. Owners want us to assure these guests that we are very very sorry, by way of appropriate facial expression and theatrically exaggerated humbling postures. That some guests no longer harbor the merest shred of humanity anywhere within the dry husk that enshrouds their miserable life, is not their fault; we must recognize that it is, somehow, at least in part, ours. We are asked to consider what we might have done during the guest's stay that could have reminded her that there is some joy yet to be had in life… and that it is not her job to extinguish it whenever she detects it flickering in others.

The owner's view, in brief, is that when we have a guest who maintains unreasonable expectations we should treat them with the greatest deference and do all that we can to make them comfortable and assure them without any doubt that they are our kind of people and are welcome back any time and, that perhaps on their next visit they will find things more to their liking.

He wants us to plead with them to return and give us just one more try. On the other hand, on the reasonable hand that is, on the rational hand, on the sensible hand, I, were it my decision, would want only to be done with them.

My myopic view doesn't allow me to see the value in having smoldering grumblers trudging around in our hallways exuding gall and taking every opportunity to accost happy guests in order to fill them with foul criticism and infect them with festering discontent. I suppose, in essence, my philosophy can be reduced to this: If you don't like it here, please go somewhere else. PLEASE. It will make it a more pleasant stay for the rest of our guests, as well as the staff. But, we have been asked never to look such a guest directly in the eye and quietly suggest that it would be a happy day when they go away determined never to return.

I realize that the bottom line nags for customers, but if I were king, I'd want to surround myself not with soreheads but with satisfied customers. It's not as if there aren't enough good guests out there. We have those. We have nice customers, and we have plenty of them. We have devoted guests, quiet, unassuming guests who like this place…who like this place a great deal… flaws and all. I'd like to give *these* guests a bottle of wine once in a while, not as an apology for how far we've fallen short of their expectation, but in thanks. Thanks for being reasonable and enjoying what we have to offer. When I do give these good people a glass of wine or two, I look around cautiously, because I'm not sure it's according to policy.

The policy seems to be: The more demanding, demented and demonic the guest, the more we must strive to lure them back. By this method the 'disgruntled' guest is always assured the attention they need and demand. They get the attention, the personal apology, the promise to do better, the thanks, the free dinner, the bottle of wine, and, despite all that, continue to stew in their own discontent.

And, just because they've checked out doesn't mean we're rid of them. After leaving us, some feel compelled to sit down in front of a computer and create some kind of overblown vitriolic rant, and paste it all over the internet. I have never seen one of these rants that didn't come across as clearly and unquestionably what it is: the railing of an unhinged malcontent.

So, I want very much to take this moment to thank the good guests who find a light bulb that doesn't work and come down to say, "If you give me a light bulb, I'll change it."

I want to tell these guests how nice it is of them to plug in something they find unplugged—though it is clearly not their job. These lovely people know how to jiggle the handle on a toilet too. They tie their own shoes and dial their own phone. They recognize good humor—even of the dry sort—when they hear it, and respond to witticism with endearing human cleverness. Their good nature runs completely through them. Better still, many of them don't seem to think I'm particularly grumpy or cranky, or if they do, they accept it, knowing that desk clerks are human too.

And none of these good people, not one, thinks I'm French.

COURTESY MOST CRUEL

I probably should have told you earlier on that I am cold and cruel, but you may have detected that already, perhaps, between the lines. It would have been fair of me to mention it however. I am cold and cruel. But, here's a secret which I have never had any desire to conceal, I'm not French. Cold and cruel, not French. My grandmother was French and she married a full-blooded German. And on the other side of the family, as my father tells it with chagrin, no matter how many times we trace our lineage back, and no matter how carefully, we're still English. How each of those brave and respectable bloodlines have contributed to creating the horrible monster that is me I don't know.

By whatever means I have gotten this way, when it comes to dealing with guests my presentation, by almost anyone's standards, lacks polish. I don't always quiver with delight at the sight of yet another human being dragging his full allotment of luggage through the front door, and I might as well admit it. Because of this, many, and by that I mean quite a few, guests are convinced that I am both offensive and French. I don't know which they think is the horse in that equation and which the cart, but, I seem to have the remarkable ability to offend complete strangers just by looking up and saying, "How may I help you?" That craft, which, apparently, comes naturally to salesclerks in high-end department stores, has come to me only through years of very hard work. I realize, of course, how offensive such a question can be—delivered properly—but, usually I am not even aware of what I have done to offend those who so eagerly choose to be offended.

That's just how dense and uncaring I am. Yes, I am the dark, impenetrable background against which the rest of humanity all twinkle like lovely little stars.

What proud creature is this stomping across the stage of Life without a single qualm, seeing only in bleakest black and chilling white, his tattered soul steeped in roiling bitterness; whose response to every disadvantage is rage, whose stance alone is a challenge, whose cold eye fixes on everyone before him in warning; and who abandons everything in his wake in ruin; and who—despite his tearful public confession—has no real fear whatsoever of God? Oh, wait, that's a mirror. So, he must be nothing more than a miserable little dark-souled desk clerk in a small privately owned French Hotel.

This idea that I am an unbearable bastard is a mystery to me for several reasons, not the least of which is that, when I worked in a similar establishment in Del Mar, I was known as *the nice guy*. Maybe it's the light in here. Maybe it's the fact that I have tiny little, close-set, squinty eyes. Maybe it's anticipation on the part of my critics—this concept that the French are difficult, coupled with this erroneous idea that I am French. On the other hand, *maybe* irritating and unreasonable people just get what they expect from me…or get back what they, unwittingly, dish up. At any rate, the most demanding and unbearable people on earth either don't like me or somehow get the idea that I don't like them (which I don't), and that my dislike for them stems from the fact that I am French. Actually though, it stems from the fact that I am honest. I realize that has no place in any business setting, especially the hotel business.

But, I remain at sea entirely when it comes to the like/don't like thing. I mean that when *I* check into a hotel, I don't give a damn, in all honesty I truly do not give one single slightly-used damn, about how the guy behind the counter treats me. I don't care what he thinks of me and I don't expect him to care what I think of him. I really want very little from him. When I check into a hotel, I'm not looking for someone to make me feel good about myself by lowering himself in my presence. I'm just looking for the key to a nice, warm, *clean*, comfortable room with all the hot water I might want to use while voicing my delight in fractured song. The desk clerk can keep his phony-baloney smiles and obsequious play-acting to himself. I don't want it, I don't need it. Give me the key; point me in the direction of my room, end of relationship.

From having been a guest myself in many hotels throughout my 60 years here on earth, I have to think it is a very small person indeed who even notices the desk clerk, let alone remembers how grievous the slight he might have suffered because the desk clerk failed to bow deeply enough upon their sudden noble appearance before him.

Of course I'd wish the desk clerk every happiness in life, if I gave him a second thought. But, I can not imagine what a desk clerk might say to me—cold, surly, indifferent, distracted, outright mean, vulgar or stupid—that would stay with me for very long, or what he could do that would inspire me to carry that wound around with me, within my breast, until after my departure when I might vent my built-up anger, at long last, in a thirty-two page diatribe on the internet.

Really, truly, such an act would say far more about me as a human being than it would about that desk clerk. There is just so much more going on in Life.

Truly though, what must the guest be *wanting* that the process of checking in to a hotel means so much to them? If some desk clerk were to wrench my bags from my hands, douse them with lighter fluid and set them on fire before my eyes, while standing arms folded defiantly across his chest and sneering, I might remember that guy. Short of that, checking into a hotel should be a non-event. But, to some guests, it means a great deal, and if they discover they don't like me during that process, it is always a GRAND disliking. It has such import that they feel they must give that feeling operatic voice.

Beyond the fact that it wounds me deeply and leaves me heartsick to think that any human being anywhere, or for any moment in time, might not find me absolutely delightful and feel themselves overwhelmed with the surging desire to make me their pet, it is amazing to me how those who have had the very briefest contact with me, can form the strongest opinions, and should be able to judge me so accurately, and find me lacking in so many ways. It amazes me.

But, unlike other forms of acute perception, I find little entertainment in their ability. I also find it peculiar that my wife—who among all people knows me best—is so thoroughly deceived. She thinks of me as a generally good-natured guy whose biggest wish is to protect her and make her happy. How is it that she continually overlooks the glaring flaws that most vile, ill-natured, sniveling malcontents, who have suffered contact with me for nearly seven minutes, see so clearly? As said, some of our guests have needs which I am at a loss to either understand or fulfill, and I don't think my participation in their delusion will help them learn anything.

When I was in college, a thousand years ago, in my junior year, at the beginning of the new session, I was walking across the quadrangle alone and was approached by a girl I had never seen before in my life. She stood in front of me and said this, "I hate you. I just thought you might like to know that."
I was completely startled.
"Really?" I said, "why do you hate me?"
"Because you are such an arrogant prick, that's why," she said and went stomping away.

As said, as far as I could recall I'd never seen that girl before in my life, yet, she had spawned and nurtured a hatred for me so profound that she could no longer keep it concealed. This was more than 40 years ago! But, at that time I was, as I pretty much am today, an inward, fairly unassuming, even timid person who feels most comfortable alone, or in the company of no more than one good, longtime, personal friend, and maybe a couple of sleeping animals. When I was a child my shyness was often interpreted as stupidity, when I was in college that same timidity was seen as arrogance, now, apparently I'm a bitter old bastard. I'm glad to see that I haven't lost the ability to offend people simply by my presence in their lives…
no matter how fleeting.

It goes on.

It is not unusual, on any given evening to hear a derogatory comment from one or another lovely gentle departing guest as they go gliding past the office door. The briefest contact with me inspires them.

"Do you have a brochure for the hotel"

"Certainly." I hand them the brochure and offer a forced smile. A funny look comes over their faces; they have detected that smiling at complete strangers for no particular reason does not come naturally to me, as it does to say, imbeciles, charlatans, salesmen, scoundrels, liars, manipulators of every sort, swindlers and politicians running for office. This, they resent. The women raise their eyebrows and tuck their chins; the men either glare at me threateningly or laugh in a superior knowing manner (which I believe is the contemporary version of throwing down a gauntlet). As they make their way down the hallway to the front door the woman comments loudly, predictably, "Well, HE's certainly in a foul mood."

In fact, I am rarely in a foul mood. Admittedly I am somewhat stiff. NO one will ever accuse me of being overly familiar. The term socially awkward might describe me, because I am not naturally a social creature and have no intentional desire to ever become one. I also prefer the sanity of solitude to any interaction with anyone needing the constant reassurance of their social position, or any other psychological assurances, which might be built upon my assumed inferiority. But, I'm rarely in a foul mood. Or, until someone comments, wrongly, on what a foul mood

I'm in, I usually dwell in a world of my own, in relative contentment.

I am direct though. I'll admit to that. Ask me a direct question and you will get a direct answer. Ask me for a local map and you'll get a local map. Some people don't seem to like that very much. I understand, but I am not an actor—I'm incapable of pretending that handing a person a map is the greatest pleasure I've experienced on any given day. Recognizing that we are not bound together throughout all Eternity, I'm incapable of pretending that every guest's fleeting presence in my life means all that much to me. The last thing I want is for my fleeting presence in theirs to mean anything to them. If they ask for a thing, say, a business card, and I hand them one, they should be completely satisfied. What more can there be to it? Yet, many go away unsatisfied.

If I could offer some advice to such guests it would be this: Rejoice, dear friends! You asked for something, and you got what you asked for; it's enough. How many things in life work out so simply? Try not to dwell on the fact that I did not plié, tour en l'air, land au point, pirouette nicely, and, with good, full extension and a large beaming, near-blinding smile, present the card to you while blinking and making gentle cooing noises. Accept the card and get on with your life.

Temporary contact with someone you feel so far superior to should never affect you so profoundly.

THAT FRENCH ACCUSATION

The French have a phrase which is literally translated, "It's not my fault", and they are very quick to use it. I find that tendency annoying. There are many things that go wrong around here that *are* my fault, and I admit as much. The problem is that many times I am misunderstood, unfairly accused, or wrongfully misrepresented, and for those things I will not accept fault. As far as the owner is concerned, these things too—whether they are my fault or not, whether I will admit it or not—are my fault. The most common false accusation against me is that I am rude.

When people think I've been rude to them they invariably also assume that I am French. I am not. Nor do I have any aspirations in that regard. What's offensive about the French, as far as I'm concerned, is not their rudeness, it's their perpetual, relentless, effervescent chirpiness. Here's the test: If French is rude, then I *might be* French; if French is chirpy, then I sure-as-Hell am not... and Hell, for me is, pretty much, a surety.

All of that explains though why people, while leaving the hotel, have been known to say:
"Screw you, you old French bastard." OR...
"Ooooh, la-la, *somebody* needs to work on his social skills." AND...
"He's FRENCH, we MUST forgive him."
For some reason these comments, each in itself a fine example of social grace, are always delivered in a childish sing-song. I don't know which I find more irritating, complete strangers screeching their distaste for me loudly

in a phony, nasal, French accent, or this idea that I am French.

Many of our dear guests are so delighted with the idea that this is a French establishment that they gush incessantly about their trips to France, their future trips to France, how wonderful France is and the glory of all things French and, most of all, how charming and delightful and just plain wonderful the French are, none of which I would argue with, for I *love* France, what I know of her. Since I was about 12 years old and discovered Charles Aznavour and, through the jazz musicians I listened to, learned of France's acceptance of blacks, I have truly believed in the very essence of my being that the French pretty much have the right idea about Life and how to live it.

Additional proof of that can be found, I think, in the fact that I carry concerns deep within me about the likelihood of that beautiful and unique culture surviving their own childlike generosity. My fear is that France welcomes, coddles and encourages far too many people who despise everything that is truly good and unique about French culture. (Yes, I realize that particular truth is neither politically correct nor socially acceptable. I also recognize that it doesn't really belong here, but I feel it must be said.)

The owner of this good establishment is the prime example our Francophile guests cite as the very epitome of the very purest French whatever. It is his charm, his cooing, his warmth, his effervescence, his willingness to stand around and chat for hours, which mark him as French. Strangely, it is my viciousness, my coldness, my indifference, my

brevity, my directness, which marks me as French in the eyes of those who have chosen not to like me.
So, where was I…?

In France, without the bonjour, no transaction will be allowed to take place. Say, 'Bonjour' and I'll sell you coffee. No bonjour, no coffee until bonjour has been uttered. It's pretty simple. It's civilized, it's quaint and, as is the French manner, just the slightest bit Gestapo-like, but it's also superfluous. When in France, I let my wife handle the courtesies. She says bonjour for both of us; I supply the awkward somewhat critical little smile of a foreign idiot traveling with his unfortunate French wife. Here, in a small, privately owned French hotel, on the other side of the world and on the other side of the counter, I expect no bonjour and ask for none. Tell me what it is you want and I'll give it to you though, offensive as that may be.

Of course that's wrong, and I know it's wrong. It offends people greatly if every interaction in a French hotel, no matter how simple, doesn't have a pleasant little seventeen minute intro and end with the kind of desperate clinging farewell that young lovers must feel within their hearts at each cruel separation.
"Pardon me, but, do you have a brochure for the hotel?"
"Yes, Madame, certainly. Did you have an enjoyable meal?
"Yes. It was remarkable."
"Well, it is our greatest pleasure to carry on amiably with you for 17 minutes while the phone rings incessantly and people gather in anxious hordes behind you, sighing loudly, grinding their teeth, rolling their eyes about, wishing only to check in and get to their rooms."

"And it is ALWAYS such a pleasure for me to drag the
simplest act out for as long as it can possibly be dragged—
but always with a delightful smile—and then suddenly
recall a question which will prolong this idiocy further
while I ignore the fact that you may have other things to do
than stand around here and chat with me about nothing
whatsoever while Life ebbs away slowly under our feet."
"Yes, and I can see that it will be impossible to get rid of
you until I turn nasty, because you just don't get the hint do
you?"
"Well, we've been coming here for many years… and I
would hate to drop the owner's name as if we might be old
friends, implying that if you don't put up with me, you'll be
canned. Let's see now… it's been, well forget that… many
years and we have always enjoyed the restaurant. I thought,
why not give the hotel a little try. I told Graham as we were
coming up in the elevator, 'Why don't we see if we can
have a little peek at one of their rooms?' Now where has
Graham wandered off to? Do you think you could show us
a room? I'm sure the accumulating throng behind me will
be pleased to wait, knowing that it is for me they're being
asked to wait."
"But of course Madame, there is nothing I'd rather do…
since no jury would understand if I surrendered to the urge
welling within me, and committed the act your mindless
prolonged nagging presence seems perfectly designed to
drive me to."

Despite all the evidence against me, I still harbor this
theory that only individuals who are themselves… let's say
trying, take this immediate disliking to me.
But, then again, maybe I'm projecting.

As said, this accusation that I am French often springs from the fact that I give direct answers to direct questions. Yet my directness is one of the many, almost countless, truly American traits, which separate me completely from the French. The owner of this hotel, (a Frenchman if ever there was one) cringes at the thought of a direct answer to any question. "It grates on the ear!" he wails. "It grates on the ear the way you... the way you, I don't know, the way you always..." An extraordinarily well-read man, a man of tremendous knowledge, with an extensive vocabulary in at least two languages (that I know of), he can't even find a word for my intolerable directness.

It's true, I don't take the time necessary to turn every simple yes-or-no answer into a bubbly reenactment of the Song of Roland. I don't load my responses with complex and convoluted lyrical constructs which might entertain the ear and draw upon the good-natured humanity, the depth of education and the quick intelligence which must certainly reside within the heart of the good and clever fellow who stands before me picking his nose and asking,
"Yew got any ice in this 'kin' joint?"
The owner's concern is that a direct answer to this man's quaintly posed question may be offensive to the man. Offensive or not, I get things done (when I'm allowed to).

So, when two trim young males come in looking for a room, I offer them a room, they ask the price, I tell them the price, and they screw up their little faces and mince away, it means almost nothing to me. I've been through this before. As they go they hold this conversation, purposefully loud enough that I can hear it.

One says, "He IS, isn't he?"
Two replies, "Definitely."
One says, "You can just tell can't you?"
Two responds, "Tell...? I can *smell* it on him."
One says, "I know what you mean. This whole place reeks of Frenchness."
Two asks, "Why are the French always so... *that way*?"
One replies cleverly, "I'd ask him, but...I'd rather have a pleasant evening."

In the American tourist's mind all French people are too cold, but that is simply not true. In the French mind all Americans are too cold, and that is, of course, undeniable. We don't either have, or even wish to have, that unconquerable French effervescence. We don't see every endless, nagging interruption as an opportunity to embrace our fellow man in warm-hearted fellowship. When we speak, our words are devoid of ever-ascending delight; our phraseology is not selected carefully in order to sing in joyous celebration of the spoken word when asking someone to hand us a 3/8-inch crescent wrench. We don't take the time necessary to turn every simple question, which might be answered simply, into a classically structured three-act drama. We just don't.

The French see us as the Hawaiians see us—soulless. Come to think of it, American blacks see American whites that way too. The Chinese, they see us all, black or white, male or female, as soulless devils. The Russians—for god's sake, the RUSSIANS—even see us as soulless. How can that be? How on earth can Russians honestly look at anyone and think them more dour than themselves?

But, all of this adds up to nothing. That every nation of earth and all the nations' peoples—yes, and even many of our own—see us as soulless means nothing. Cold or not, real Americans serve their purpose in this world, if only to be despised by others. Soulless or not, we get things done. There's a wall that needs tearing down? Hand me that goddamned sledge hammer, and step aside. Leaky sink? Hand me that pipe wrench and don't stand there looking at me, I don't need any assistance. Getting things done—I've been roundly criticized for that particular character flaw, by the owner... in those times when he doesn't need a thug to do his dirty work for him.

"You, you sneak around in your quiet way and you do what you have to do without making a sound and then you sneak back again into your little rooms..." He has actually said this to me. For this—for traveling without herald, fanfare, and entourage—and for accomplishing things—without mulling, pondering, extensive debate, bleeding from the eyes, saintly speculation and prior approval—no thanks should ever be given, and believe me it isn't. I sneak out, like a mouse, I do what I must do, I sneak back into my little rooms, like a rat, and I receive no thanks. For this— for being the only one around here who could possibly accomplish certain brutish tasks—expel some entrenched belligerent from a room for example—I stand accused.

That I am an American male is a criminal accusation for which there can be no defense however. For this alone, but for so much more, I should probably be hung.

HOW TO GET TO THE BASEBALL PARK

I honestly feel that there are some, albeit admittedly very few, good people in this world who do not (yet) speak French. I'm not claiming that I am one of them. But English is a legitimate language and many people, especially here in the United States of America, feel no qualms whatsoever in using it.

In France I feel most comfortable not pretending to speak a language which I do not speak. But, here at home, others sometimes insist that I do, or apologize for the affront… which I never do… which is an additional affront. Stubbornly, I refuse to apologize for not speaking French.

One afternoon I arrived at the office and squeezed by Mme. Bertrand (owner, along with her husband), the dog-in-law, a woman, and her husband, all standing around in a clump, cluttering up the hallway. The woman was speaking in what I recognized as a highly respectable version of American-learned French. Madame, who is somewhat hard of hearing, was nodding her head very convincingly, as if she might actually be hearing many of the words. I slipped through and found my spot behind the desk and started looking at email. Then I heard Madame say in English, "Edward would know about that. Perhaps you should ask him." She stepped into the office with this woman, and the woman's devoted little husband followed. The woman then did something I would never think of doing in someone else's office, and which I do not like our guests to do, she came around to my side of the desk.

Then, she began speaking to me in French, saying, in essence, "We wish to go to the stadium. How do we get there?"

Madame interrupted her, saying, "Edward speaks English." The woman responded crisply in French, "I speak French," adding to me, "as you have seen."

At this point this woman already had me considering another occupation.

I asked, in English, "You want to get to the ball park?" The woman said, "I speak perfectly good French..." and proceeded to again ask me, in a kind of proud, crippled French, the most convenient way to get to the ball park. "Well," I said, in English, swiveling in my chair to face her, "the easiest way is to take the bus. You can take any bus heading south on Stockton Street," and I gave her directions how to get to one of these buses. "If you get off at the train station, you'll be within two blocks of the ballpark," I said. "But," I added, "I don't think you can get tickets to tonight's game." The game had been sold out for days, and I thought she should know that in order to avoid disappointment. Mission complete, I swung away from her and went back to a much more pleasing aspect of my work, data entry.

"We HAVE tickets," she snapped.

And, since there was nothing to be said to that, I said nothing. I was careful not to raise my eyebrows. But she wasn't finished.

"What if we wish to take a taxi?" she asked coldly in French.

"Well, I'd go right here to the corner, that way you can catch them heading in either direction." I said in English, and returned again to my work. The woman and her meek little husband vanished. The air of unhappiness which she had generated remained behind however; as I'm sure she would have had it.

Forty minutes later she reappeared in front of me—again on my side of the desk.

"Is that something you simply do not do for your guests?" she demanded in English.

I was at a total loss. "Don't do..? I'm sorry…What do you mean?"

"Is calling a taxi for your guests, the guests of your hotel, something which you simply will not do? Or did you think we just walked in off the street?" she snapped.

"I'll be glad to call you a cab if that is what you would like…" I stammered, confused. "But, why do you think it is something we don't do?"

She stared at me bug-eyed for a while, then, taking a deep breath she said, "You know, when we checked in here this morning, the Chinese girl behind the desk, and her daughter, were BOTH perfectly charming. And, we've found the maids ALL charming, and just everyone we've come into contact with here has been so courteous and so charming. This lady that I was talking with, IN FRENCH, this afternoon, was one of the sweetest most charming people I've EVER had the pleasure to speak to. She was JUST charming in EVERY WAY…and considerate and helpful."

"And…" I urged her to get to the point.

"And YOU. You refuse to speak to me in French; you tell us to go climb on a bus like peasants; you tell us to go off somewhere and flag down a cab on our own; gesturing wildly, dismissing us like you can't be bothered. We are *guests* here. Apparently you thought we were bums who wandered in off the street. That's the way you treated us. You treated us like peasants."

During this tirade, her husband stood silently behind her, hands folded in front as if to protect anything that might remain of his manhood.

"None of what you have just said, Madame," I said calmly, "is true. You asked me the easiest way to get to the ballpark and I told you. The bus is the easiest way; it is the way I would go myself if I didn't walk there. You asked me about cabs and I told you where you might easily get one. It is what I would do myself, if I wanted a cab on a Friday night. On Friday nights the cab companies in this town don't even answer the phone, let alone take advance reservations. If you had asked me to hail you a cab, I would have done that. Instead you asked me, 'What about a cab?' If you want me to call you a cab now, I'll do that, but I don't think they'll answer. If you want me to hail you a cab, I'll do that. But, what you say is simply not true."

Her husband was grinning behind her back and nodding in agreement, but I could tell that I couldn't depend on him to rally with me at that moment, or testify on my behalf when that damned woman's strangulation in our office came to trial. He had to put up with this kind of nonsense every day of his miserable life... apparently in worm-like silence.

"You said," and here she mimicked me (and did a pretty good job of it too; though I thought her delivery should have been a lot more condescending, and she could have held her chin up higher), "*You can't get tickets to that game.*" Well, I'll have you know that we HAVE tickets to that game; my SON got them for us months ago."

Now, the chin was up.

"Would you like a taxi, Madame?" I asked.

"We would like a taxi," she said, turned briskly and headed toward the front door. She waited at the door for me to open it for her, and, in an effort to match her childishness, I waited a bit before I did.

I followed her and her husband outside and stepped into the traffic to troll for a cab. She stood at the curb and shouted at me, "You treated us like peasants!"

I stepped back on the curb and faced upstream. "I didn't treat you like peasants," I said. "Right now, you are acting like one," I murmured, mostly into the wind.

"Go to hell!" she screamed shrilly at me.

"Et Voila!" I said.

"Go to hell," she screamed again.

"Thank you for making my point," I said to myself.

"You just lost a lot of customers!" she snapped.

"Madame, I have lost nothing," I told her. "Madame Bertrand—that lady you rightly said was so sweet and so charming—she is owner of this place. If anyone has lost a lot of customers, it is her."

"And that's too bad too. This is all because of YOU," she shrieked. "It's too bad because I *teach* Advanced French in a college in Boston and I could have sent A LOT of customers your way, but not now." She raised her chin in victory. "Not now…"

"Lady," I said in perfect, precisely enunciated American English, "I'm just a desk clerk."

I thought about adding, "I'm paid an hourly wage to put up with peronnelles like you. Depriving this establishment of your pompous, knock-off, wanna-be French friends is perhaps the nicest gift you could give us." Though tempted, I kept those thoughts to myself.

"Well, I'm going to write the owner a letter," she said.

"Make it a long one," I told myself quietly, "They seem to like the long rambling, incoherent ones."

"I'm going to tell her what a bastard you are."

"Believe me, Lady" I said, "she already knows."

As a cab pulled up I opened the door for them, but didn't wait for them to get in or to shut the cab door; I was pretty sure I wasn't going to get a tip. I bowed a little bow and went back in and to the office.

Of course all of this was very very wrong. And I knew that no one, least of all the owner, would see it as the heroic act that it was. So, for my actions here, I should, first, have my tongue removed… and then I should be hanged. As a final act of defiance, I'll wear jeans and sneakers to the hanging, and utter my last gurgling words in English.

MEAN, OLD, and FRENCH (no doubt)

One evening a rather stiff, grayish, raw-boned gentleman and his pasty-faced, dumpy, little, disapproving wife stopped in front of the desk and the following exchange took place:

"Can we make arrangements for dinner in your restaurant this evening?"

"Certainly, what time would you like?"

"Seven. The name is Wilson."

"Thank you, Mr. Wilson; we shall see you at seven."

That was the conversation in its entirety.

Ten minutes later I picked up the ringing phone and Mr. Wilson is on the other end. He's what we might call *hoppin' mad.* He tells me boldly, he's shouting actually, "My name is Wilson and I want to cancel our reservation in your restaurant!"

"OK," I say calmly.

"I'm sorry I have to do this, because it looks like a good restaurant."

"OK," I say.

He takes a deep breath and then blurts out, "And I want to tell you why."

"OK," I say.

"Because," he says, "frankly, I've never been treated with such rudeness in all my life."

He then slams down the phone (an act which no one on earth would ever consider rude).

So, first a challenge and then a little story.

I admit confusion. What was the nature of the affront? Clearly it was the kind of slight which can not, apparently, be easily either forgiven or forgotten, but what exactly had I done? It requires more imagination than I possess to understand how my words could have offended this gentleman so profoundly. Perhaps it's the sort of thing that can only be seen by others, from outside. Maybe I'm too close to the matter to see it clearly.

That aside, here's the challenge. I challenge anyone, ANYONE —the greatest actor on earth—to deliver these lines in such a manner that it would generate that *id*-gentleman's response. The lines are: "Certainly, what time would you like?" and "Thank you, Mr. Wilson; we shall see you at seven."

As I recall it, I maintained my very best faux smile during this brief exchange. Perhaps this he found offensive. Perhaps there should have been more trembling on my part, or greater joy, maybe something in between. He'd never been treated with such rudeness *in his entire life*. That imbecile must have been 60 years old, and had never been treated with such rudeness in his entire life. Does that mean he never once visited the Department of Motor Vehicles, or never once set foot in a hospital emergency room, or an auto parts store, or flagged a cab, or spoke to a cop? Let me be clear on this. I was not rude to the guy. However, I would really like to have a second shot at it.

Now, an excerpt from an old children's bedtime story springs suddenly to mind:

...And then the monster purred, 'Certainly, what time would you like?' 'Seven,' the little girl stammered timidly and hugged her teddy bear more tightly in her arms. Then the great big French (no doubt) monster growled, 'Thank you, we shall see you then.' With those cruel words she began to trembled and shake all over. Who wouldn't? She trembled and shook all the way home. The outrageous treatment she had received at the hands of that mean old, French (no doubt) monster gnawed on her. She had NEVER BEEN SO INSULTED in all her life!

That cruelty gnawed on her until the fundamental dignity that dwells within us all filled her with a great righteousness. AND she picked up the phone. AND she cancelled her reservation. Better still, she told that mean old French (no doubt) monster exactly why *she was canceling.*

It's sad to say that the little girl's cancellation had no effect whatsoever on that mean old, French (no doubt) monster. Sometimes the cruelty of this world is beyond all understanding.

Sometimes what is perfectly clear to everyone else is beyond my understanding.

A woman calls asking, "Do you have any rooms with 18th Century antiques?"
"No," I say, and for what I would consider a good reason: we don't.
"None of your rooms have *any* 18th Century antiques?"
"No."

She can hardly believe it.

"None of them?"
"No."
"Not one?"
"No."
"You don't have even one room which has 18th Century antiques?"
"No."
"Well what do they have then?"

Here's the challenge: answer that question in any way that will satisfy that woman. Maybe you can. I couldn't.
"Well thanks a LOT!" she says and hangs up.

I thought I detected a bit of sarcasm in the way she said it.

NOT THE OWNER

One evening a nice French gentleman, while riding up in the elevator with me observed, "You are not French."
And I replied, "No. I am not French."
And he said, "But this is French hotel."
And I said, "Yes, this is a French hotel."
He said, "Are you the owner?"
I said, "No, I am not the owner."
He said, "But the owner is French, no?"
And I said, "Yes, this establishment has been owned by the same French family for 46 years."
"And you are not the owner?"
"No. I'm not."
"Ah…" he says.

The next day I am called into the owner's office because the nice French gentleman has complained about me.
"I don't understand the nature of his complaint," I say. "He asked me if I was the owner of this place and, since I am not, I said so. I'm sorry, but honestly, I do not understand the offense in that."
The owner sighed and looked at me. I know he was hoping I would get it, but I didn't. So, I continued with my explanation.
"The guy asked me if I was the owner, and since I am not the owner, I said that I was not. THAT'S his complaint?'
"Yesssss," he sighs.

"I mean, he comes to you—the owner—complaining that I—who am not the owner—when asked if I am the owner—denied being the owner? Is that it?"

He looked at me for quite a while.

"I'm sorry," I said, "I don't get it."
"Yes, but, it is the WAY in which you say these things."
"How many ways can you answer the question, 'Are you the owner?' You can say 'Yes', which in my case would be a lie, or you can say 'No' which in my case would be the truth, and that's what I went with. I don't see how that can be construed as an affront of any sort."
"It is the WAY in which you say these things," he said again. (We both shook our heads I'm sure.)

So, here again I must raise the challenge. I challenge anyone to say, "No, I am not the owner," in such a way that it would offend any reasonable person. Believe me, if you can offend someone by employing those few words, you are a master, and maybe you should be working in government instead of wasting your time doing real work.

All that aside, the actual owners of this hotel have not only managed to turn a run down old hotel into a lovely and inviting little place to stay, they've managed to do something that perhaps every hourly wage earner on earth has dreamed of doing; something rarely attained by anyone other than in the movies; after working here for many years, they bought the place. But, I wasn't around during any part of that good, hard work and it would be shameful of me to claim that I had any part whatsoever in their success. So, I'll stick with, "No, I am not the owner."

I realize that answer may upset some people.

PHILOSOPHICAL DIFFERENCES

The very first time the elevator broke down while I held the front desk alone, at this small, privately owned French hotel, I quickly dashed off a notice on the computer, printed out 6 copies and ran up to the top floor. Taping, neatly, one copy on each elevator door, on every floor, I came traipsing gleefully down again. In my mind it was a job nicely done —and quickly.

My note said, "Elevator Out of Order. The repairman is on his way." In small print, at the bottom in a trim red cursive, it said, "We apologize for the inconvenience." A very short time afterward—I had just barely gotten my feet up onto the desk and my hands interlaced comfortably behind my head—the owner bellowed my name from inside the darkened cavern of his elegantly, yet whimsically appointed office.

When I arrived in front of his reasonably gilded desk he waved the notices, bits of tape still attached, under my nose accusatorily. "What are you doing?" he asked, apparently tormented in a manner only other eternally suffering saints might fully appreciate.

"I'm letting our guests know that the elevator has broken down, that we are aware of it, and that we are doing what we can to see that it is taken care of. Oh, AND," I added smugly, "that we're sorry." Knowing me, I may have raised a finger heavenward to put a fine edge on this final point. That was, after all, the part which marked me as true small hotel administrative material.

He stared at me for a long time with what could only be assumed was the deepest disappointment. It had that look about it. And when it became clear from my eager glance that I didn't get it, he sighed. It was the sigh to end all sighs, full of resignation, hopelessness, despair; a true French sigh. I watched as he collapsed in upon himself, surrendering completely to the crushing brutality of Fate which had saddled him with this burden which no mere human could possibly be expected to bear. He could not, nor would he ever, understand why he had to explain these things to me.

Clearly, from the idiotic smile upon my face, I had no idea what the problem was. While I waited to be informed I raised my eyebrows in mutton-headed expectation, a sign of complete cooperation. I was willing to learn.
(In those days I was still willing to learn.)

"But it is too COLD!" he moaned at last, taking yet another arrow in his already shaft riddled heart. "This notice is too cold." He tossed all of the notices, tape still attached, onto his desk. He sighed once again wearily. "Why don't you say…We lament the fact that we are forced to announce that our old and EXTREMELY devoted friend, this fine and rare instrument, this conveyance, this, this… elevator, which has served our guests for more than EIGHTY YEARS without complaint of any unreasonable sort, has just now taken it upon himself to rest until he should regain his former strength, and once renewed, he will, of course, continue to serve us in the dedicated manner in which we have become…" He stopped. (Those were not his exact words, but that was the essence of it.)

He took off his glasses, rubbed his weary eyes, replaced his glasses, looked at me. It was no use. He shook his head. "Well, you see what I mean," he said in a way that conveyed his own doubt. "But, this," he picked up and waved the notices at me again, "What you have written is too COLD! Go, and re-create something with some style, with some, as you say, flair, with some evidence of the touch of the human spirit. For you, I would say, put something down that informs our guests of our deep concern in this matter."

This may have been the first time (I do not know for certain but, for certain it wasn't the last) that he looked at me fully convinced that I was a complete idiot. At that moment, the poor man knew, without a doubt, that I had not a clue about what it meant to work in a small privately owned French hotel. Perhaps that moment was also the first time (not the last) that I looked at him convinced, without question, that the poor man had some very strange ideas himself. It was, by any measure, an awkward moment for us both.

Both bullheaded, single-minded, self-reliant and self-convinced individuals—and I think, underneath it all, both crushingly timid by nature—we glared at each other for a bit across the chasm. Then, both being reasonable, fair-minded, and relatively good-natured, we looked at each other a bit longer, in cold ringing eternal silence.

In that moment I believe that each of us was making a serious effort to discern any sign of intelligence behind the other's thinking, the other's actions, or even the other's existence.

Being a man of 15 years more experience, he could find none in me sooner than I could find none in him of course. So, I continued the search long after he'd reached his unfortunate conclusion about me.

He hung his head and rubbed his eyes, while I stood there feeling stupid. When he looked up again, there was a message in those eyes. You will never know my suffering, they seemed to say. Then, resigned, he swiveled around in his chair, giving me the back of his grey but fully-thatched head. I stood there awkwardly for a while longer before walking out of his office… since I had no gun. But, even if I had one I probably could not have decided which of us to use it on. I guess it would have been a matter of either justice or compassion, but I'm not a deep thinker and both of us would leave good wives behind.

As far as I could determine it was merely a philosophical difference. He thought, in this case, that when guests come thundering down to the office, stands there seething in the doorway with their hands on their hips and fire in their eyes, demanding snappishly, "Is the elevator running?", a good reply might be, "Well, you know…Come in, come in. Sit down. This is why we have these nice chairs here. Please. Come in. This question which you have so simply, and, perhaps a bit directly, asked is not answered so simply. We must properly consider first that, well, yes, he is an OLD device, an ancient device, sure this may be, and a mere machine, but he is a well-meaning machine—he has our best interests at heart, this machine—and, yes, like many old machines he needs from time to time to…"

On the other hand, my feeling is that when a guest appears glowering in the office door with smoke pouring out of his ears and demands, "Is the elevator working or not?" a good answer might be "Yes." or, depending upon the circumstance of course, "No." In many cases a reasonable response might be, "Let me go see what I can do about it."

Just as an aside, I've noticed that when I'm running up and down the steps, sweating like a mule and playing with high-voltage electricity trying to restore the elevator, our guests wait with exponentially building impatience an unmasked discontent. When the task is finally complete and I stand at last before them drenched in sweat, huffing and puffing still as I hold the elevator door, they look at me as though I was the guy who broke the damned thing, rather than the guy who fixed it. This irritates me—but that is a character flaw of mine. I'm not meek enough, and perhaps for this I should be hung.

At any rate, all this stuff about the owner thinking me an idiot or me thinking him deranged—though perfectly true—does not really get us anywhere. It is enough to say that the owner and I have many philosophical differences when it comes to the hotel business. His view on guests, the rooms, the staff and what is and what is not a priority around here, are largely a mystery to me. His view on these things, I can not understand. My hope is that after I explain them to you, if I do a good job, you won't be able to understand them either, but, at least you won't be able to understand them from my point of view.

At first, with many of these little differences, I could not predict what his response would be, but very soon I would learn that whatever I did was wrong in his eyes. That was one of the very first lessons I learned here at this small, privately owned French hotel: if I went right, he would sigh as though wounded afresh and say, "Why did you not go left?" If I went left, he would lower his head as if resignation were his sole remaining option and say, "Why did you not go right?" If, because of that lesson, I made no decision, I would be told, "You must wrest authority and take action." But, if I made any decision on any matter no matter how insignificant, I'd be overstepping my bounds, and it would be seen as an affront to his position as owner.

I admit that I have natural, deep-seated difficulty adjusting to that kind of nonsense and, fairly shortly, began to resent it. I am, after all an intelligent being, Soon I found myself in the position of an intelligent being with plenty of responsibility but absolutely no authority. And that is not only frustrating (and by that I mean infuriating), it is also infuriating (and by that I mean endlessly frustrating).

In reporting these little philosophical skirmishes to my dear wife I feared that I may have portrayed the owner too frequently in an unfavorable light and, one time, I actually expressed that worry by saying, "I don't want to always cast myself as the reasonable one..." I looked at her only to see that her lovely lips were pressed so tightly together that they had actually begun to tremble. I was surprised at how much effort it takes to hold back a simple phrase like, "There's very little chance of that."

OUTSIDE INPUT

It doesn't take some guests long before they feel they must offer their very good and kindly advice about how to run a small, privately owned French hotel. These guests are, in my opinion, misinformed about the nature of what a hotel provides. One such creature, having stayed here twice, and during that time observed all that one might need to observe in order to know much more about running this hotel than the owners—who have been at the helm for almost 50 years—came to me one day and said, "This place is cute, but you really should keep it up."
"Ha ha ha!" I laughed. "I do not know what business you are in, Madame," I said, and here I stood up "but I would not dare to tell you how to run that business." I realized immediately that I had stepped over the line, but she had stepped over that line first.

The lady was appropriately shocked… and she looked it. "Well, as the owner, I just thought you might like to know what your guests must think while looking around your building."
"I am not the owner, Madame," I said, "I work here for an hourly wage." "But," I thought, "If I WERE the owner, you would never stay here again."

She did one of those fluttering palms on the chest routines, accompanied by the stiffening neck, the well-tucked chin, and the bulging eyes, before departing without another word. It was too bad too; I wanted to hand her a plunger and send her off to room #302 where she might sharpen her insights through hands-on experience.

I would be the last to attempt to deny that I am a loose cannon. It would be easier for me to do a double-back flip from a standing start than to deny that what I sometimes say to such miserable people is out of bounds—guests though they may be. BUT, I like to think that when I go off it is usually a matter of justice. Just for the record, the owners have put in more than 46 years of continuous effort to raise this building from the relative squalor they found it in to what most of our guests perceive to be a delight in almost every way. No one here, and especially the owner, would deny that this place could use another 46 years of carefully orchestrated tinkering to bring it to the heavenly vision he must harbor in his mind, but if the only thing you see in this lovely little hotel are its faults, the most glaring fault resides within you.

That's the way I feel.

Though it was kind of this woman to hide her real feelings behind such a caring, cautiously worded statement, my good wife—who has lived in this building for every minute of those afore mentioned 46 years—was deeply and rightfully offended.
"Does she think that my parents walked into this hotel at the height of its perfection and simply stood by and watched as it went to wrack and ruin?"

This was one of the very few times I've seen my dear wife truly angry at anyone other than me. I attempted to calm her by saying, "Ah, guests!" The appropriate response would have been, "Ah, guests indeed!"… but she was too angry to play along.

"Ah, guests," I repeated with waning hope, but she didn't budge. She was FURIOUS.

Other guests seem to think they should have a say, not just in how the hotel is handled, but in how we handle our personal lives as well.

The woman leaning casually in at the door of the hotel office one evening, smiled and told me, "I have to tell you this. From the very beginning, my husband and I were *totally* against you marrying Miss Bertrand. But, now— now that it's been, what... ten years—we're starting to believe that it might actually work out." She smiled prettily as she continued to lean upon the doorpost.

I must have looked startled... but that didn't stop her. She went on in a most amiable manner. "I mean, really, think about it. Sylvie is intelligent, well educated, well traveled, young and beautiful and French..." She stopped short of saying, "and then, of course, there's you." But, she stood there long enough to be sure that I filled in those blanks myself. She smiled when she saw that I had gotten the point. I smiled a crumpled little smile in return, and, because I've been told it's unacceptable for anyone in any business setting to lash out with the sort of cold, merciless response that was careening around in my mind at that moment, said nothing.
I think I deserve some credit for that.

I had no idea who that woman was. As far as I could tell, I had never seen her before in my life, though she claimed to be a regular guest at the hotel.

Still, until that very moment I would have never considered passing judgment on *her* marriage. Now, I thought that perhaps her poor husband could have married someone with a bit more discernment.

That aside, it's interesting to see how many people think they must offer us their advice... and never ask us in return for our opinion on the way they run their lives. So virulent is this infectious idea however that one can not help but play around constructing a reasonable, measured and (of course) completely unacceptable response. I thought that what I had said to one guest spontaneously was good enough to remain in the final composition however. Meanwhile I tinkered it into a kind of perfection.

And, so, here we have it. Best delivered standing with steely eyes, the full rant goes something like this: "You've been in this establishment for three minutes, Madame, and you are now prepared to offer us a variety of ways by which we might improve ourselves. I must say that I am impressed. I am sure the owner will be most pleased to receive your recommendations, and eager to put them each into play. Before you go, first, thank you, and second—this is unofficial, of course, just between me and you, just between us—I do not know what business you are in but I can tell you this, I would not dare to tell you how to run that business. It would not even occur to me."

Of course, while working on that rant, I realized that the only workers who can get away with treating their customers with such utter and total disdain are government workers, auto parts store clerks, the entire so-called medical community, lawyers, bankers, used car salesmen, bus drivers, the airlines folks, cab drivers, plumbers, electricians, contractors of every ilk, department store clerks, shoe salesmen, grocery store clerks, secretaries, dentists, washing machine repairmen, the cable and satellite people, stock brokers, waiters, wranglers, accountants, welders, tow truck drivers, musicians—both amateur and professional—panhandlers, cops, politicians at every level and certified financial advisers. The rest of us must handle our customers with kid gloves.

But, I think it can be agreed by anyone in almost any line of business that things would just be so much easier and a whole lot more pleasant if business could be conducted without the steady annoyance of having to deal with customers.

In this business I think we make a serious mistake by calling our customers guests; it only gives them ideas.

THE POWER OF NAMES

A peculiar thing occurs almost immediately after someone meets the owner face to face, shakes his hand, and hears him say, "I am the owner of the hotel, how may I help you?" From that very instant forward these people feel as though they are entitled to special treatment. Once they have shaken the man's hand and looked him in the eye, they are transformed; now they are no longer mere customers, now they are close personal friends of the owner. And, I really wish he'd stop that.

Naturally, close personal friends of the owner can not be expected to lower themselves to book a room through normal channels, through a desk clerk for example, like everybody else; they cannot book a table in the restaurant through the front desk like everybody else; close personal friends are entitled to speak directly to the owner, and only to the owner, concerning such highly personal matters.

When the lowly, despicable, and devious desk clerk suggests over the phone that the owner is not immediately available for taking their reservation—the heavy unspoken hint being that he might have other things to do—his close personal friends always insist. Denied, they hang up smartly. But, these very special people call back shortly, and demand again to speak to the owner. And, each time they call back they insist more coldly, more firmly, and therefore they must, necessarily, be turned away more coolly, more casually. Or at least that's my method.

And it only gets me into trouble.

When someone tells me they have known 'Marcel' for years, what they are really saying is that they want a discount. They want to make arrangements through the owner because he's a nice guy and generous and a soft touch. They don't want to deal with me because, well, then they would be demoted to the disgraceful level at which everyone else must dwell. Why, I have asked my wife, are so many of the people who claim to be this man's close personal friends so cheap? To this she has no answer, but the smile of wisdom plays across her lovely lips.

At any rate, it is not unusual for one of the owner's close personal friends to call on a night when the hotel is solidly booked to demand a room for her own out-of-town guests, or, on a night when the owner himself could not be seated in the restaurant, demanding a table for eight. And it is not unusual for me to deny them something which we do not have and therefore can not provide. That's predictable. More predictable still is the sharp tone they take on when they again insist upon that thing which we can not provide.

When they are denied, they grow huffy, they grow regal, they rise up to aristocratic heights and they not only insist, they *absolutely insist,* upon speaking to the owner. They call him by his first name. They've raised pigs together. Perhaps I don't understand my position here... or how tenuous it might soon become.

Inevitably it comes to this:
"You refuse to accommodate me?"
"Madame," I say, "Tonight I would have to turn away my own mother."

"Is Marcel there?"

"He's not available. What can I do for you?"

"Is Marcel, *the owner*, there?"

"He is, but he is unavailable. What can *I* do for you?"

I say this whether the owner is here or not, available or not. I think the idea that he is here but I am preventing them from getting to him gives my response the kind of cruel twist every close personal friend of the owner really should experience at least occasionally.

"I want to speak to *the owner*. Tell him that Marguerite Witherstone wishes to speak to him." This demand comes from a woman who once sat in his office for three hours and forty-seven minutes chattering before—now, that they are such good friends—wheedling a donation of free room and dinner for two out of the man. But, it's for the High-Republican French Alliance of Animal Protection Advocates United, so who can quibble with that? Or, perhaps she once looked him in the eye at some cocktail party, smiled wildly—and somewhat crazily—and, while shaking his hand warmly, read his name tag and declared how wonderful it was to meet him at last.

"He is not available," I say.

"Have Marcel call me back immediately," she commands.

It is just as though she truly believes that the owner has the time, the inclination, the saintly patience and, here's the real kicker, the ability to accept her reservation, whereas we, the lesser idiots of this crew, can not or will not or… well, who really knows what goes through the minds of the service class (?).

In all of this she is wrong. The owner has neither the time, though he makes it, the inclination, though he suffers through it, or the ability, though he pretends to remember how it is done, to take reservations from people, no matter how irritating they may be, in those times when we simply cannot accommodate them. This has been proven many times both in the restaurant, when parties of 30 show up and there is only a startled look in the owner's eyes; or when, for example, a famous French crooner arrives and there are no rooms for himself, his lovely leggy young wife, and his somewhat less lovely, nearly as leggy, but only slightly younger, daughter.
(There's a story there. I'll tell you later.)

But, whether this great man can take a reservation or not, he CAN NOT create rooms where there are none or, in the blinking of his great eye, expand the dinning room to accommodate some pushy old broad and her snotty poseur friends who speak infantile French badly but with pomp. In brief: the owner is neither a carpenter, nor a magician.

Though I would love to turn this woman away, just because I think God himself would applaud my actions, I would never do so if we could find her the room or the tables that she so charmingly demands. What would be the point? We are in the business to rent rooms to guests and fill tables with eaters, no matter what section in Hell is being happily prepared for their inevitable arrival there.

In this case—in this instance, where a close personal friend of the owner demands a room that we do not have—I am instructed by the owner to call Mme. Witherstone back and tell her regretfully, nicely (this is repeated as if I might be hard of hearing) NICELY, that, had it not been for the helicopter crash and subsequent fire on the fifth floor we would have gladly accommodated her guests. And, (this he repeats while raising one cautionary finger to get my attention) AND, that we, of course, look forward fondly to seeing her again, and very soon, perhaps on some other happy occasion.

So, I call.

"Mme. I am calling to inform you that I have spoken with the owner and we regret to have to tell you that we can not accommodate your guests this evening. I can offer you the number of a reservation service however which will help you find some other nice hotel for your guests."

"Is Marcel there?"

"We have no rooms, Madame."

"I want to speak with Marcel."

"He can not help you, Madame. We have no rooms."

"I insist that you put me through to Marcel!"

"I regret, Madame, to say that the owner has gone home for the evening."

"I just spoke with him," she lies unconvincingly.

"Yes, I know Madame, but the owner has left."

"What's your name?"

"My name is Philippe, Madame."

"Well, Philippe, the owner will hear about this."

"Of that I am quite sure, Madame. Would you like me to spell Philippe for you?"

We have no rooms. It is a simple statement of fact, but she can't seem to understand the concept that underlies those four words.

On my part, I cannot understand at what point the communication fails. I find myself looking for a way to introduce her to the concept that all the rooms are taken. I'm sure that Ms. Witherstone thinks that I am hiding something from her—that we have rooms and I won't admit it. But, why would I do that? Honestly, if I had a room I would rent it to her just to be done with it; to get her out of my ear and off my back, and, for a little while at least, out of my life.

Many (believe me, MANY) people who don't get what they want think that I am being a bad desk clerk; intentionally uncooperative or unhelpful or unkind or unnecessarily cruel or—the greatest slight of them all—indifferent to their needs. When I say we don't have valet parking or we have no rooms with whirlpool baths, or we don't provide a wake-up service which involves three or more staff members, dressed as druids, dancing in circles while either singing a medley of ancient Celtic songs beside their bed or softly reciting selections from Ayn Rand's Harvard speeches on The Martyrdom of Capitalism, they seem to think I'm being purposefully difficult. They truly believe that *we do* offer these services, but, due to my belligerent nature, I wish to selectively deprive them.

And, the fact that we do not offer these things, in the eyes of the guest, that's probably my fault too.
(Now, where did we leave off?)

"Well, PHILIPPE, Marcel will hear about THIS!"
You know, if the woman were here, sitting across from me at the desk, I could do something about that.

I would rise up in my full magnificent and most frightening aspect, and order her to her feet. Then I would, escort her across the hall to the owner's office where I would kick in the glass paneled French doors and demand of a somewhat startled, but clearly unimpressed, owner if he would like to go with us to look at some rooms. He would decline of course; he is perhaps the busiest man I have ever met.

After obsequiously returning the shattered doors to their closed position, as best I could, I would once again assume my most frightening demeanor, and, by the ear if necessary, escort the lady to the elevator. She would, naturally I suppose, be trembling in fear on our way up to the top floor, where I would hold the door and tell her to get out.

I would then escort her by the elbow to the very last room in the back of the building and insert my pass key and open that door and force her (and here I think a gun might prove useful) at gun point if necessary, to look in there and determine for herself if that room was occupied. Once that was determined, from there we would move on systematically opening each and every door—maid's closet, maintenance room, guests room—skipping none, until she determined, to her own satisfaction, that all of the rooms on that floor were occupied.

We would then make our way down to the next floor, and in the same manner continue until every door on every floor has been opened, and every room inspected and determined by her, to her own satisfaction, to be occupied.

When we arrived back at the office, after having together inspected every room in the place, she would no doubt collapse into a chair across the desk from me.
Or that's how I imagine it.

As she sits, blank-eyed, stunned, motionless, exhausted, I feel confident that I have made my point. She now understands the meaning of the phrase, *We have no rooms.* I give her some time to absorb it.
"So, what have you learned here today?"
"That you have no rooms."
"And what did I tell you before… when you first came in?"
"That you have no rooms."
"That means that we have no rooms for you, or for your out-of-town guests, we have no rooms for ANY of the owner's close personal friends. We have no rooms for anyone. We have no rooms for the Queen of Sweden, we have no rooms for my own dear mother, should she suddenly appear before us on our doorstep with her luggage in hand, pleading, lip all a-tremble, for mercy. We have no rooms." I turn both palms heavenward and shrug. I smile. "We have no rooms. But the real lesson, and I think this is a good lesson for you, Marguerite," I say, "is that you can not have everything your way all of the time. If you have until now, those days are over."
"Thank you, Philippe," she says as we stand.
"It's my pleasure, Madame," I say bowing slightly.
"Thank you, Philippe," she says patting my hand. Now I see, as she looks up at me, that tears of joy are flooding her once vindictive eyes.
"You are quite welcome, Madame."

She leaves a much improved human being.

I like that ending better than, "Well, PHILIPPE, the owner will hear about THIS!"

MY PEOPLE-HANDLING SKILLS

One time, a gentleman had locked himself in a room and refused to vacate on the day he was scheduled to depart. He challenged the desk clerk—a tiny Asian woman—to extricate him. The barricaded guests reportedly told her, "I'm not leaving and you can't make me!" When she explained that the hotel was fully booked and we needed that room for incoming guests, he challenged her yet again saying, "I ain't leaving, lady!" I guess he thought he was playing a part in a gangster movie.

By the time the desk clerk decided she needed my assistance in the matter, the gentleman had been holed up in his room for several hours, and had dug in. Now he was refusing to even pick up the phone. She was upset because the guests who were slated to occupy that room had arrived. She had cleverly convinced them to go have a cup of coffee "While the maids make up the room." At this juncture she called in the scourge of God, the misanthropic desk clerk, the equalizer, me.

The misanthrope, playing his cello with eyes clenched tightly in anticipation of the inevitable interruption, but just then surrendering to a kind of musically inspired reverie, received the call from the tearful young lady with something other than reasonable composure. Flying to the front desk with fiery breath he demanded, "So, what's the deal?" The facts were these: When she had called up around noon to ask when the gentleman would be checking out, he said he'd decided to stay. When he was informed that the hotel was booked and he would have to leave, he said, "That's unfortunate for you, because I've decided to stay another day or two." When it was explained to our guest that the hotel had no other room to offer him, he laughed. He said, "I ain't leaving and you can't make me."

The misanthrope looked at the file to verify that the gentleman was in fact scheduled to check out. He looked at the man's credit card pre-authorization, which seemed to confirm that he had been expected to stay only so long. He looked at the guy's signature at the bottom of that file, to verify that the man had agreed to the length of stay. Then he went over the facts again with the desk clerk.
"And what did he say?"
"He said he's decided to stay another day," wept the clerk, "or two...!"
"And what did you tell him?"
"I told him that the room was rented, that we had no other room to offer him and that he should please leave."
"And what did he say to that?"
"He said, 'I'm not leaving, and I'd like to see you try an' make me.'"

This challenge rankled. And although he did not welcome such a challenge, the misanthrope was up to it. He slipped quickly and easily into his belligerent mode and, climbing the stairs three at a time, went up to the room and knocked gently upon the door.

The guest, assuming it was the tiny, quiet and, by this point thoroughly intimidated Chinese girl who he'd been shoving around for hours, bellowed loudly from within, "Yeah? What is it?"

The misanthrope answered in his deepest, gruffest, and, possibly, his most sincere voice, "I'm here to tell you..." He let his sentence trail off into silence. It was a ploy. The guest came to the door and opened it. He then found himself confronting the misanthrope face to face. This was a mistake.

"Oh, I won't be checking out." the guest said in soft, even, dulcet, courteous tones. "I've decided to stay on." He smiled sweetly, he blinked innocently. Suddenly the scoundrel was Lillian Gish.

"You ARE checking out," said the misanthrope, neither smiling nor blinking, though courteous to a muchness.

"No, but I've decided to stay over," said the guest smiling in a most becoming manner. He was the perfect gentleman. The perfect gentleman was assuming that the misanthrope had not heard about the threats he'd directed at the desk clerk throughout the afternoon.

"Did the woman at the front desk tell you we are fully booked?"

"Yes, but I've decided to stay on."

This is the perfect example of what we in the hotel business call customer ploy #387. In that ploy the guest is demanding, condescending, belligerent, abusive, vulgar, loud and cruel to the maid, the desk clerk, the server— anyone that he perceives to be an underling—and when someone of apparent authority appears before him he has the composure, the wit, the courtesy, the charm of a diplomat representing Heaven's highest angelic order, the Seraphim.

"Did she tell you we have no other rooms available?"

"Yes."

"In fifteen minutes, you will be out of this room," said the misanthrope, "or I will personally remove you from it."

The guest just looked at the misanthrope.

"Do you understand what I've just told you?" the misanthrope asked the guest.

"What's your name?" demanded the guest, drawing himself up to his full height and employing what he assumed was a genuine threat. This is an example of customer ploy #4326. It has NO effect on a misanthrope.

"My name is Edward," said the misanthrope as cold as ice, "and I hope you understand that this room is rented; we have no other rooms to offer you; you were scheduled to check out this morning; you WILL be leaving this room, and you will be leaving this room very soon. I'm coming back up here in fifteen minutes and you had better be gone."

The guest responded by saying, "OK, *EDWARD*," and slammed the door.

What the guest did not understand was that any attempt to have the misanthrope fired would be futile. He did not understand how many hours, days, weeks the owner of the hotel had spent on his knees in devout prayer begging whatever gods there be that the misanthrope would quit or run off with an exotic dancer, or be run over by a bus, be discovered dead in the morning or just simply disappear. He did not understand that if it were possible for the misanthrope to be fired, the misanthrope himself would welcome the firing. He did not know about the large bottle of excellent champagne being kept perpetually on ice just for that occasion... somewhat peculiarly, by both parties.

So much of this sort of thing had happened so many times over so many years that the owner was either immune to it, or so very weary of hearing it that it no longer got through to him. Or, perhaps, his poor heart was, by now, so scarred that there was no longer any surface area available for fresh wounds delivered by reports of the misanthrope's always surprising misanthropic behavior.

This tale reveals yet another of my many character flaws: when a guest barricades himself in his room after threatening a fellow worker I don't play games with him, I simply oust the son-of-a-bitch. So be it.

This of course is wrong. I believe the official policy requires that we first apologize profusely, then we find him another room at a more expensive hotel, supply him with limousine service to that hotel, and send him an elegant little thank-you note suspended by a golden ribbon from a bottle of our finest champagne. That evening, we then call him up to see that his new accommodations are suitable, that he is comfortable and happy, and ask if there is anything further we can do for him. In the very rare chance that the matter involves me in any way, I would be expected to wash his feet with my tears before carving the word 'RUDE" into my forehead using a rusty nail, and hanging myself in Union Square.

In our current example, the desk clerk this gentleman had chided and derided and threatened would be expected to go over shrouded in sackcloth and, bowing deeply in humility and shame, surrender the teddy-bear of her youth while lamenting, "I hope he brings you as much joy as he once did to me."

I think that by just tossing him out into the street like a bag of garbage I may have missed a few of those steps.

The following day, as anyone might have predicted, the owner called me into his office where the guest who had refused to leave (and therefore had been ejected) sat quite comfortably with a smirk on his lips and one leg thrown up over the arm of his chair as if he might own the damned place. I thought that was a nice touch on his part. The casual approach while being reprehensible is always nice. Perhaps there's a future for him in politics.
"You owe this gentleman an apology," said the owner.
"No I don't," I said without blinking. This revealed yet another character flaw of mine: my tendency to refer from time to time to reality.

Unlike the owner of the hotel, I do not feel that the employees of the hotel are always wrong and the guest, no matter how pushy, belligerent or insane, is always right.
"Oh, but you do…" said the owner of the hotel.
"In point of fact," I said, "this gentleman owes one of our desk clerks an apology." I started to delineate the details of the situation but I was cut short.

"It doesn't MATTER," said the owner. He raised both hands palm out. "None of that matters. What matters is that this gentleman was rudely, RUDELY, removed from his room here, where he was staying as our guest, and…"

Our guest was sitting—slouching—watching this scene unfold with great amusement. Here the loyal servant in me tried once again to insert some of the details necessary for anyone to understand the incident and thereby judge it properly. And here again I was cut short. No facts, no truth, would be allowed into this trial.

"It DOESN'T MATTER. He is our GUEST. He is our GUEST. Don't you understand?" With this the owner of the hotel removed his glasses, lowered his head and rubbed his ancient eyes. Then, replacing the glasses he smiled weakly at the gloating former guest—and waved me away. The gloating former guest waved bye-bye.

A few moments later, the owner was at the office door with the still gloating former guest—a grown man who challenged our tiniest female desk clerk to eject him—grinning like a hyena beside him. The owner personally showed the guest to a seat and instructed me, renegade desk clerk, to write out a gift certificate good for one night's stay at the hotel. And when this guest got up to leave, the owner was standing in the hallway with the usual apologetic bottle of wine, and presented it to the much abused gentleman with humility. He then shook the man's hand, escorted him to the front door, opened the door, and held it open as this wonderful human being, this fine and noble creature, our dear guest, departed. *Yes, yes, come back soon and barricade yourself in one of our rooms again!*

Meanwhile, in the office, I wept. I wrung my hands and I wept. "Dear God," I prayed. "please get me out of this madhouse."
What are we to learn from this lesson?

I do not know.
In the name of God and all that is holy, I do not know.

The owner has it correct. I do not understand. And, I
believe he knows by now that I never will... because this
sort of thing is beyond understanding as far as I am
concerned.

I know, of course that this indicates yet another flaw in my
character and perhaps the best thing for everyone involved
would be for me to hang myself at the very next available
opportunity; I'll add rope to my shopping list. But, in the
meantime, anyone who insults the innocent while I'm still
around will receive no champagne at my hanging, and, they
will have to lick their own boots, because I don't think the
owner will attend that joyful event.

TROIS et TROIS AGAIN

Let's start with this:

Nothing ever happens around a hotel unless something else is already happening. All that is required to set this law in motion is to attempt to undertake the completion of any task. Any task, no matter how simple, will be interrupted by the emergence of three additional tasks, each of which will, in turn, be disrupted before completion by some other matter. That's the hotel business. For a man who was taught, believes, and has always lived by the admonition, 'Take one thing at a time, work on it until it's complete, THEN move on to the next task', the hotel business is almost insufferable. Our world, this stupid frantic world in which we find ourselves today, IS insufferable for anyone who likes to do things well and completely.

Nothing inspires people to check-in like the arrival of six or seven others also wishing desperately to check-in. It is as though they all wait out there on the street until a large enough throng has accumulated, then, in mock innocence, they pour in with a built-in reason for discontent.

A great joy awaits me almost every day when I arrive at the office, as I survey the ever-accumulating wreckage left behind by our gentle guests; door knobs, towel racks, remote controls, various broken parts from table lamps and curtain rods. Most of these things don't require immediate attention, but, there on the desk I also discover notes on the various toilets that need plunging. That has a certain immediacy to it, I admit. But, it's not the kind of immediacy that might have demanded a solution while the maids were still around and available for the task, nor the kind of immediacy that would require the person at the desk *before my arrival* to handle it; it's the kind of immediacy that requires me, as soon as I arrive, before I do anything else, to find a plunger, go bounding upstairs, and take care of things—it's that kind of immediacy; the kind that falls only to me.

Without getting too much into it, let me but say this: my grandmother lived in the same house for one hundred and four years and not once in all that time did her toilet ever need plunging. But, that is a different and distant world, a fond memory. Additionally, I have myself lived on this planet for more than 60 years and not one time has any toilet in any of the many places I have lived required plunging due to anything I myself may have done. I think this remarkable record is due to my habit of limiting my use of 'paper' to less than thirty feet for any single visit and never having even once considered flushing a rubber boot. In this world however, the world in which I find myself now, toilets need plunging every day and it is always an emergency... which can wait for my arrival.

The guests are always, in every single instance, amazed by my poor, and by that I mean surly, attitude concerning this task. They are, each and every one of them, shocked to discover that I am not perfectly delighted to glove up and go to it. That I do not arrive fluttering just above the floor on wingéd feet, that I am not whistling a merry little tune while I sloppily glunch away inside their bathroom, and that I depart without a cheery little word and without thanking them for the honor, without the idiot-like bobbing and grinning they apparently expect, seems to always take them by surprise. I'm sure the owner hears of these things and I am sure it upsets him. I'm sure it makes his heart sink. It makes my heart sink when I'm raising some warm delicacy on the end of a fork toward my open mouth with eager anticipation, and I pick up the screaming phone to discover someone in-house telling me that their toilet has overflowed. Nothing makes the phone ring as quickly, as incessantly, as lifting a laden fork toward your mouth.

Our dear guests always tell me about their overflowing toilet in an indignant tone, as if someone else must have sneaked into their room behind their backs and done this horrible thing. In that tone I discern the slightest hint that they suspect that I might be the culprit. This distancing of themselves from any responsibility in the foul matter irritates me.

Perhaps it is this that these wonderful people detect in my manner when I arrive at their door with a look that would make Beelzebub cower. Admittedly, for this I should be beaten with sticks.

I'm sure the owner would prefer that I shrug on a tuxedo for the occasion; arrive at the door bearing a small bouquet of freshly picked wildflowers, while singing cheerful little French folk songs slightly off-key. Maybe I could develop some kind of clever little trick with the plunger which would amaze and delight our dear guests as I enter their bathroom, and come up with some humorous asides to shout from within while I work away, or a clever little quip that I might drop upon completion of the task, something pithy, memorable, something to tell their friends back home. "And then, after the grisly task was done, upon emerging from the fray, he said..."

What frustrates me about much of this is my attire. As a faux-gentleman working in a small privately owned French hotel I am expected to represent the establishment in a particularly respectable way when it comes to attire. So, when I go in to work I am nicely fitted out in an expensive French dress shirt—you know the kind, with the tail cut far too short to stay put and the buttons held on with a single stitch of the frailest ethereal thread. I sport an imported silk tie, personally selected and hand-delivered from Venice by the owner himself, dress pants, dress shoes, perhaps from France; I am cleanly shaven, cut and combed, with sparkling teeth and a fresh effervescent attitude. I look good because it is demanded of me.
I suppose I would feel good too, if that were anything I was familiar with; the attitude thing I'm still working on.

I'd like to make something clear: I don't mind being bubbly if I have a reason. My imminent arrival behind the desk at this hotel somehow fails to supply me with the reason I apparently need. I know too much about what is bound to come next.

Nonetheless, there I am each evening, singing a little song as I stroll down the hallway to work, looking good, smellin' good (most of the time)—*this is the day that the Lord has given us*—feeling ever so slightly apprehensive, knowing that what awaits me is usually forty minutes of sweaty manual labor... doorknobs and toilets... toilets and doorknobs. By the time I am done, the shirt has pulled free, it has lost a button, the tie is wet (despite my years of experience), I am sweaty and disheveled, the fine shoes are scuffed, the pants are stained and wrinkled, what little hair I have left is messed up, my sparkling teeth are nowhere in sight, I'm tired, I'm irritated, I may be scratched or freshly bruised or bleeding, and I am in a foul mood. I certainly don't love guests as much as I might have earlier; I know too much about their personal habits.

At this point I have six hours left on my shift, and that I fail to twitter joyously like a little bird when guests arrive in hordes before me, all anxious to check-in immediately— and expecting to do so simultaneously—seems reasonable enough from my point of view.

Of course, they don't like it. I wouldn't like it either.
I feel compelled to say however that no reasonable person would disagree with me on this: doorknobs should stay on and toilets should flush. It would be a better world.

On the other hand I know that people don't like to have someone glaring at them, when they arrive at their hotel after a long, tiring day behind the wheel, or a worse day suffered at the hands of the airlines which, these days, have somehow developed an even greater distaste for their customers than banks, politicians or even healthcare professionals.

However, presented coolly, correctly—had they the time to sit and listen to my plea—no reasonable person could see any other side to these matters than mine. Presented diplomatically, and by that I mean in a way that I am

144

absolutely incapable of, they'd be nodding their heads in agreement and commiseration. As it is though, when they sit down to face me, they have no idea what I've been through (what my problem is, as I've heard them say), why I glare, why the courtesy I offer them is brittle and maybe just a bit chilling. In my heart of hearts, I know, of course, that there is no reason why these poor arriving innocents should be exposed to the likes of me. And, truly, it would be better for everyone involved if I were simply hung.

But, I'd probably be bitter even at my own hanging.

BEHIND THE MASK

One time a nice, pleasant guest came in, sat down, and asked me a simple question, which I answered maybe a bit abruptly, perhaps just a little snappishly. I followed up quickly, apologizing to her for being rude, but hinted at the unmitigated stupidity, demands, cruelty and completely incomprehensible behavior I'd suffered that day at the hands of others. Locked in a never-ending war, we sometimes have a tendency to paint non-combatants with the same broad brush we use for the enemy.
"I'm sorry," I said, and I meant it.
This wonderful and intelligent woman replied, "That's OK. I understand. I deal with people on a daily basis myself. You were just being human."
I said, "Well these days, being human and being rude are seen by many as the same thing."
She laughed, and then cautioned me, "A hardened demeanor shields the vulnerable heart."
May God bless that good, kind and insightful woman throughout eternity.

Of course we were treading on thin ice and we both knew it. In the hotel business there is an unspoken code that disallows ANY genuinely human interaction between the staff and guests. Infringement is called *being overly familiar,* and it is nearly as great a crime as indifference.

Somehow, so far, I have managed to avoid being overly familiar with any guest.

MS. SWEETE

As Fate would have it this woman's name was Sweete.
She had checked in, in the afternoon, with her cowering
little female companion, and they had been in their room
until sometime in the evening when I got a phone call. The
cowering companion told me that Ms. Sweete wanted
something which we do not have—I forget the specifics,
and by the time I finish telling you this, you will too.
Whatever it was, I explained that we did not generally
provide that and, knowing me, I suggested a place where
they might go out to obtain it. Ms. Sweete took the phone
from her friend to make the demand herself, but we still did
not have what we did not have 10 seconds earlier. Ms.
Sweete said a few select foul words to me before hanging
up. So far, everything was normal.

About twenty minutes later Ms. Sweete's meek little
companion showed up in the office door and apologized to
me for the way Ms. Sweete had treated me. I told her that
was OK, there was no reason why she should apologize for
her friend's behavior and, when I said this, the poor woman
began to sob and shake all over. She turned pale and I had
the feeling she was going to pass out, so I asked her to
please have a seat.
"I can't. If I'm gone too long she's going to come looking
for me and that won't be good. You don't know how she
gets."
"Oh, how does she get?"
"She gets really angry and… believe me, you don't want to
know. I really… I really… I have to get back."
The woman sounded completely frightened.

"Are you going to be OK?" I asked.

"Oh, sure, she uh… she just gets really angry and it can get out of control for a while, but uh…"

The woman's lip began to tremble and then she said this, "I'm scared to go back, but I'm even more scared not to."

"You're frightened by her?"

"Oh yes. I have good reason. You don't know her temper."

After much consideration I asked, "Why are you traveling with someone you're afraid of?"

The poor woman broke down in tears.

I comforted her as best I could within the parameters of my employment here, but took one step beyond, saying, "You don't have to stay with someone you're afraid of…"

She looked at me somewhat startled and left in a hurry.

About twenty minutes later Ms. Sweete called down and asked once again for the same thing that she'd asked for before—which we still could not provide—and, once again I told her that perhaps she could get it at Walgreen's or at a corner store.

She showed up at my desk less than a minute later, a short, fat, red-faced woman with tiny little eyes. Her trembling companion was in tow. Ms. Sweete stood in the doorway with her hands on her hips and shaking her head, said, "I shoulda known. I shoulda known. Just as I expected, some old, white asshole with a tie."

I said nothing to that.

"You don't have anything to say?"

"What would you have me say, Madame?"

"What would you have me say, MADAME?" she mimicked me. "I'd have you say anything instead of that."

I said nothing to that. I remained in enforced silence.
She said, "Are you just going to sit there staring at me, you flaccid old prick, or are you going to say something?"

She sat down heavily across from me. "If you can't think of anything to say, I want to speak to somebody who can. Is there a manager around here?"
"I am the manager at the moment."
"There's no one else around? No REAL manager?"
"I am the manager."
"I want to speak to a REAL manager. A REAL manager. Is that phrased simply enough for you to understand?"
"There's no one else…" I said, "I'm it."
"OH, so suddenly you're the only one around? I want to speak to your manager!" she demanded.
"I am the manager, you can speak to me."
"Well, then I want to speak to the owner."
"The owner is not here."
"Oh, suddenly there is no manager, there is no owner, all I have to speak to is this useless old white asshole who can't think of anything to say but, I AM THE MANAGER, I AM THE MANAGER… Is that it?… everybody's gone home and left you in charge?"
"What may I do for you?"
"You can get someone in here with some balls, that's what you can do for me. I want to speak to somebody who can get something done around here."
I said nothing.
"Oh, so now you can't think of anything to say to that either? Is there ANYONE around here other than you— ANYONE with some brains, with some balls, who isn't going to just sit there blinking at me like a fucking idiot?"

"I'm it."

"You're it alright. You are the most useless piece of crap I have ever had to deal with. You can't answer a single fucking question; the manager and the owner have both mysteriously disappeared leaving some old white asshole in charge; and HE can't even respond to a simple question."

I couldn't believe any of this was real. I just sat there looking back at this disgraceful human being.

Meanwhile, in the doorway behind Ms. Sweete, her skinny little companion stood cowering. She was in tears. Sweete turned to her and snapped, "Is this the guy?"

The companion nodded.

"You," she said, pointing at me, "better learn to stay the fuck out of other people's business." She instructed her companion to go back to the room and the woman fled.

"I should call the cops, that's what I should do," she said running her hands over her jaw. "I should just call the cops."

"I'm not entirely sure what the problem is, but if you want me to call the police, I'll do that for you," I said.

"I should. I should call the fuckin' cops."

"Would you like me to call them?"

"Yes. Yes, call the cops. Call the fuckin' cops and let me speak to them. It'll certainly be better than sitting here and watching you stare at me. DO IT! Call 'em!"

So I called the police.

Quite naturally I suppose, when I finally reached them they wanted to know why I had called. It was a good question. I wasn't really quite sure myself.

"Well, I'm a desk clerk at a hotel," I began, "and we have a guest here, and she asked me to call you."

"The guest is there with you?"

"Yes."

"What is the nature of the problem?"

"I'm not sure."

"You're not sure."

"No, she asked me to call you."

"Can I speak to the guest?'

"Sure."

I handed the phone across to the woman.

Her side of the conversation went like this: (sweetly)

"Yes? I have no idea, Officer. We were just sitting here talking and he said, 'I'm gonna call the cops.' I really have no idea, Officer. There's no problem that I'm aware of. As I said, we were just sitting here and he decided he needed to call you. No, no problem at all. I could not possibly even guess."

Then she extended the phone to me and said, "They want to speak to you."

"Yes."

"Do you need police assistance?"

"No."

"Then I want to advise you. Do not call here if you are not in need of police assistance. OK?"

"Sure."

"You sure?"

"Yes."

"Don't do it ever again."

"So. Asshole," she says to me after I hang up, "I hope you're happy." And she gets up, and she walks out.

And even as she goes, I know that it is only a matter of time before the letter arrives, and I am called into the owner's office.

Why did I not try to make this guest feel more welcome? Why did I not do whatever I could to accommodate her needs?

In the letter she will say that I was rude of course, and I guess perhaps I was. As for calling the police, I can offer no explanation; I'm still confused about that myself.

SHORT STORY LONG

If you have been following these tales in some supposed chronological order and have been seeking a place at which the *caring* has finally been driven completely out of me, then you have now reached that place. And yet, we are not halfway home. Nonetheless, this is a true and accurate accounting of the event which broke the camel's back.

I'm in the office, I get a call.
A man says, "Do you have someone staying there named Bell?"
I say, "Yes, let me put you through to her."
He says, "Wait, wait wait. I don't need to talk to her. I just found her cell phone in a cab."
I say, "If you want to bring it by here…"
He says, "No, no no. She can come by here and pick it up; I'll leave it at the front desk." He gives me the name of a motel on Ninth Street and Harrison. He gives me the phone number.
I say, "OK, I'll tell her. It's very kind of you."
END OF CONVERSATION

I call Ms. Bell's room; she's not in; I leave a detailed message.

The phone rings. It's the same guy. He says, "Hello, I just spoke to someone there and he didn't give me his name."
I say, "That was me, my name is Edward."
He says, "It's very important that they come here and pick up the cell phone, I've left it at the front desk."

I say, "Thank you. I'll give her the message when she gets in. It's kind of you to…"
He says, "We're just an old retired couple and we're here for only a few days…"
I say, "I'll give her the message."
He says, "OK, because we're just old folks, retired, and tell that customer that we found her phone and it's at the front desk."
I say, "I will tell her. I'm sure it'll be OK."

The phone rings two minutes later. It's the same guy.
He says, "Is there someone named Edward there?"
I say, "That's me."
He says, "You say this is a hotel, but I don't think you're a hotel. You answer the phone that way, but how am I supposed to be sure this is a hotel?"
I say, "This is a hotel, we've been here since 1910."
He says, "Well, Edward. I think this is a scam. I think you are using this Bell person and the taxi driver to pull off a scam. And I want to tell you that I have just called the police and have given them your name."
Well, what can I say to that? I say nothing.
He hangs up.

He calls back again saying, "Is this Edward?"
I admit as much.
"Well, Edward I want to speak to your manager."
"There is no manager. I'm the only one here."
"Then I want to speak to the owner; I want to speak to somebody other than you, Edward."
"I'm the only one here."

"You say you're a hotel and you say you're the only one there. You won't let me speak to a manager, you won't let me speak to the owner. I don't even think you're at a hotel. I think this is a scam. I think you and the cab driver are in on it together." He hangs up

Meanwhile Ms. Bell has walked in and is sitting in the lobby. I've tell her where she can pick up her cell phone and she makes arrangements to get a ride to this other motel.
He calls back, "I've reported your little scam to the police and they're on their way over there right now, Edward. I thought you should know that."
"Thank you," I say.
"I'm also filing a complaint with the Better Business Bureau on Monday. But in the meantime I'm sending the police over there right now."
"Thank you," I say, "I look forward to their arrival."

Ms. Bell goes over to the motel and picks up her phone. Passing by the front desk when she gets back, she stops to say that the guy at the front desk of the motel was glad to see her. He told her that "the old man had called down 17 times" to see if she had picked it up yet.

Next day, the owner of this hotel has my wife in his office and he's complaining to her for forty minutes about something. When she emerges I ask her what it was about. It was about a nice old man who called and left a somewhat lengthy, perfectly calm, perfectly courteous, genteel message on the owner's voicemail saying that someone who called himself Edward was "rude and uncooperative ,

refusing to help him get in contact with a guest." This
very kind and gentle old man was attempting to return a
lost item, which he had found, and someone named Edward
had decided to do everything possible to stand in the way in
order to prevent that kind gesture from happening.

So, I'm called into the office and roundly chastised.

When I get out, in confusion and desperation, I call Ms.
Bell and tell her that I am being railroaded by this idiot
cell-phone motel moron guy and IF she would consider
shedding some REAL light on the issue I'd appreciate it.
She says, "Gladly," comes down immediately, knocks on
the owner's office door and enters. She emerges 10 minutes
later. I have no idea what she has said to him.

The owner comes into the office and speaking, not to me
but to my wife, in French—in my foul American presence
—rambles on and on for minutes on end with escalating
fury. He concludes his rant by saying, in French, "Edward
is not entirely clean in this matter."
I say to him, in English, "This is complete NONSENSE!
Some idiot calls here. I take down the information he gives
me…" But, I am cut off.
"It does not *matter*," he says, trying to dismiss anything
that might cause him to veer off in the direction of either
truth or fact or rational thought.
I continue, "He ASKS me to pass on this information to a
guest, which I do…" I am cut off again.
"None of that matters, you are not without guilt in this," he
declares.

"Yes," I say, "I am. At what point am I guilty of ANYTHING? I don't even understand the nature of the accusation."

The owner says, "You don't understand? Let me repeat it. You are not entirely pure white in this matter."

I say, "Yes I am. I did NOTHING wrong. And," I say, "It's unfair for you to expect me to defend myself against the weird, contrived accusations of some IDIOT."

"Puh!" he says, dismissing everything I say.

"I did nothing to that man. I took a message, which he asked me to, and passed it on to a guest, that's all I did."

The owner stares at me for a bit.

I continued, "I still don't understand the nature of the crime."

The owner throws up his hands and as he's walking out of the office he says, "You are not entirely innocent in this matter."

I'm left thinking, I still don't know what the matter is.

So, I've thought about it. I've ranted and raved and cussed really loudly, while pacing around screaming in front of my poor trembling wife, as I tried to work my way through this, with hopes of discovering exactly what I was being accused of. If *you* can tell me, I'd love to hear it.

It is ridiculous, unfair and completely INSANE to expect me to offer any defense against some bizarre accusation leveled at me by some unknown idiot calling from a cheap motel on the other side of town. But, that's only my POV. Perhaps, because this is a French establishment, when the bastard offered to send the cops over to have me arrested,

I should have offered him dinner-for-two and a bottle of our most excellent wine.

After having thought about it for a very long time I can see the owner's point of view however. I see it clearly. Believe me, I see it clearly. And, it is this:
Given the choice between believing an obviously insane unknown making bizarre and outlandish accusations about a conspiracy between a desk clerk, a guest, and a cab driver, OR believing a man who has given you 12 long years of dedicated service, anyone would naturally side with the obviously insane unknown accuser.

For my inability to recognize the reasoning in that, I should probably be hanged.

It would make the same kind of sense.

THAT BLASTED NOISE

Innocence is a wonderful thing, and some truly innocent people stay at this small hotel from time to time. Some are so innocent you wonder how they survive in this world; others are strong in their innocence.

One evening when I held the keys, the head waiter called up from the restaurant begging me to hurry downstairs. When I got there I had to cover my ears because there was an eardrum piercing screech coming from somewhere. "What the heck is that blasted noise?" I shouted, "What the hell is that?" The place was packed and the waiters were too busy serving to stop and offer suppositions. As they scooted by they shouted, "Find it. Stop it." I think one of them, a newer employee, may have added, *please*.

I checked the stereo…nothing wrong there. I went out into the restaurant proper and looked around. The guests all seemed anxious for a solution. Some were pointing at the various electronics which they thought might be the source. It had to be something up near the ceiling; that's where we hang all the electronics. I looked up at the lights, the speakers, various wires and devices hanging around up there, then went out quickly and got a ladder. I propped it up near a speaker and climbed up and put my ear to it. As I went through the restaurant systematically eliminating speakers, lights, motion detectors, anything electronic, the diners offered their encouragement. I had their full support in my efforts to put an end to that horrendous shrieking, and before long we were all old friends. They seemed to enjoy watching my quest.

And, I have to say, I was taking it well for a guy who, in general, hates electronics, dislikes ladders, doesn't like people all that much, and has no desire whatsoever to be the center of attention. I was actually being kind of human about it. I can not tell you why the process of tracking down a screeching noise in a restaurant buzzing at full capacity didn't irritate me, but it didn't. Even more peculiar, I found myself playing to the crowd a bit, gesticulating widely; only the power of mime could cut through that piercing sound.

After methodically eliminating every high wattage light, motion detector and speaker on high, I climbed down and shrugged in an exaggerated manner and scratched my head. My audience seemed as confused as I was; they pouted. They encouraged me to continue though—the noise was not letting up and it was unbearable.

A very nice old gentleman sitting near where I'd last propped up the ladder looked up at me, smiled, and asked in a friendly manner, "What are you looking for?" He'd been oblivious to the whole affair.
"I'm looking for the source of that screeching sound!" I said loudly.
"What sound?" he asked.
"You can't hear that screeching sound?" I bellowed.
"No."
I motioned for him to look around at all the other diners, some with their hands over their ears, some with fingers inserted, and he said, "I can't hear it." He tapped his ear. "I can't hear a damned thing."

160

I was standing not two feet from this old gentleman and I could hear it clearly. In fact, I could hear almost nothing else. It seemed louder than ever. "It's right around here somewhere," I said. "I can't believe you can't hear that." His soft-spoken, frail, little, flower-like wife said, "He can't hear a thing with that new hearing aid."

That sound was definitely coming from somewhere around there. It seemed to be coming directly from their table, but all I could see was a small vase of flowers, their plates, some silverware. I closed my eyes, I cocked my head, allowing my ears to direct me. It was certainly coming from that table. I leaned over the old man, saying "Excuse me…" and when my ear passed near the side of the man's face, I discovered something horrible. That horrendous screeching was coming out of the poor man's head.

"Oh!" declared his wife suddenly with delight, "Good gracious, Harold, it's your hearing aid!"
"What?"
"IT'S YOUR HEARING AID!"
"What is?"
"THAT AWFUL SOUND; it's your hearing aid!"
"It can't be, I just had the battery changed."
He took the hearing aid out of his ear, looked at it, and turned a little wheel. The screeching stopped completely.

The diners were all delighted. And just like in a bad movie, they applauded, they cheered. "Good work!" one gentleman shouted. All eyes were on us, so I bowed very slightly and said, "Our next show will be at 9:30 when we'll try to determine the source of all this light in here."

As I took the ladder back to storage I had to admit that I felt a warm glow for my fellow human beings, and a special glow for that old gentleman and his charming wife.

The next morning I approached life expectantly, though I bore the suspicion that the seed of brotherhood which had fallen so unexpectedly upon the rocky ground of my cold misanthropic heart would never be allowed to sprout. So, I approached each event of that day with caution.

Several days later, when that fine old couple checked out, there was still a quiet little whistle coming from the man as he sat down.
"I'm afraid we have to check out tonight, because we'll be leaving early in the morning," he shouted.
"Oh, going back home?" I asked.
The man looked confused and turned to his wife and said, "Do I look Chinese to you?"
She pointed at her own ear and said, "It's that new hearing aid; we'll have to get it checked out when we get back to Indiana."
"That's probably a good idea," I agreed.
"You'd think a new hearing aid would work better."
"I would think so," I said.

Throughout all of this the old gentleman was looking back and forth between his wife and me, pretending to be irritated. "You two keeping secrets from me?" He winked. She pinched him playfully. "And," he said, getting back to business, "I think we should turn in one set of keys tonight since we won't be needing them." He reached into his pocket and took out a set of keys and handed them to me.

I laughed out loud as soon as I saw them. They were the owner's keys. We'd been looking for them for days.

"I never could figure out what this other key was for. The wife has only two on her set," he said.

"This one's to the owner's office," I said, holding up the keys, "this one's to the wine cellar."

"Ha, ha, sure they are," he laughed.

"These are the owner's keys." I said, and they both laughed.

'Yeah, I bet," said the man. "Why didn't you just give me the key to the safe while you were at it?"

"Seriously," I said, "These are the owner's keys."

"What?" he said.

"THOSE are the owner's personal KEYS," explained his wife pointing at the keys.

"I heard him," said the man, "I just don't think it's so. I think he's joking with us, Aida."

I took the keys. I stood up. I motioned for them to follow me the short distance across the hall to the owner's office. I held up one key for them to see. I inserted that key, gave it a twist, and with a showman-like bow pushed open the door to reveal all the wonders inside the owner's whimsical little office. The couple came forward and looked in. They looked at each other astounded.

"I will be danged," said the old gentleman with delight. He patted me on the shoulder.

"Do you want me to show you the wine cellar?" I held up the key to that place.

"I WILL be danged." He shook my hand vigorously. "We had 'em all this time…" he said.

"Oh my goodness," she said astonished.

"We had the keys to the whole joint…" he said. "We could've been runnin' the show by day and drinking good wine by night… *on the house!*"

"That'll certainly be a story to tell our friends," said the lady.

It turned out to be a story to tell my friends as well.

IS THERE A MAN SO SELF-DECEIVED

Is there a man on earth who does not honestly feel that he can run the organization he works for every bit as well, if not better, than the guy who is actually running the damned show? As the French say, it is only natural for a caring and thinking man to feel this way. Since I am not a thinking man, it's the caring part that nags. Oh, if I did not care I would be a free man.

Of course, we are all wrong, those of us who think we can run the organization we slave for better than the guy who makes continual irrational, unreasonable, risky, idiotic and embarrassing decisions at the top. For me to think that so many things around here should work or should be corrected or could be improved in any way, only reveals how little I know about the hotel business and how much I lack in blind loyalty and unquestioning obedience to an undisclosed, perhaps not yet fully-formed, vision.

A man comes into the office and hands me a doorknob. "The maintenance guy already put this back on once today… and once yesterday as well," he tells me in a jovial manner. He looks old enough and kind enough, and intelligent enough to converse with, so I try.
I say, "You know my grandmother lived in the same house for one hundred and three years and no doorknob ever came off in her hands."
He says, "Your grandmother lived here?"

I retract my *intelligent enough for conversation* evaluation. I said, "No. My grandmother did not live here."

"You just said she lived in the same house."

"She did, she lived in the same house."

"The same as what?... You mean she lived in this house?"

"THIS is a hotel. She lived a house."

"But you said she lived in the same house. I thought you meant this house."

"This," I said, calming myself... calming myself... "is not a house. This is a hotel. My grandmother never lived here."

"And so, what was the point about the doorknobs?"

"The point was that, in those days, they made things so that they would work not so they would fail."

I'm having difficulty here because I am contractually obliged to put up with this kind of thing. Oh how I long for the presence of mind to weigh my answers according to the questioner's ability to understand me.

"This one hasn't failed," he says, "it's just come off."

"I'll replace the doorknob," I say, taking the thing from the man. I'm not even slightly tempted to explore the fine differentiation he sees between a doorknob which fails and one that has come off in someone's hand. This is one of those things that I can not see clearly, and, any attempt will only give me a raging headache. One time, long ago, in my past, I recall being confused as to why anyone would climb up into a tower and simply throw himself off.

"We're not in there right now," he tells me and looks around at his wife as if to prove the fact. I am tempted to say, 'I can see that', but instead say nothing. I wince because, in certain situations, it's difficult for me not to say what I am thinking. It is almost always the best alternative however.

"It just needs a little extra tweak," he says.

"Believe me," I say, "it'll get some tweakin'."

"So, you think you can fix it?"

"I can."

"Cause the other guy couldn't."

"He hasn't had as much disappointment in his life."

These two good solid Americans look at each other as if this might be the most oblique statement anyone has ever made, and then they shrug and waddle off together in their brand new, snow white, predictably squeaky sneakers. Believe me it'll get some goddamned tweakin'.

One evening we had a little temblor—a big jolt actually— and a guest calls down and says, "Did we have a little shake just then or is it my imagination?"

I said, "If it was your imagination then you have a pretty powerful imagination."

He says, "Why's that?"

I say, "Because everybody in this town felt it."

He says, "So, it wasn't my imagination?"

I say, "If it was your imagination, please rein it in."

He says, "Why's that?"

I surrender, "Yes. We had a little jolt just now. It was not your imagination." I try not to sound like I'm suffering too much, but I really want to know why this man drives a better car than I do and lives in a bigger house.

He snaps, "Well, thank you!" and hangs up.

Somehow he understood that part perfectly.

I'm lost either way; I'll be hanged if I'm too direct, and hanged if I attempt to make human contact.

My very dear wife says I need to calibrate my response, and I think she's right. I guess I don't know how to do that though. As it turns out I was not this gentleman's favorite hotel employee, and I have to admit, he was not my favorite guest of all time.

My favorite guest of all time won that esteemed title by uttering three words. He'd arrived late at night from Chicago on the Zephyr, and stayed four nights. When he came into the office to check out, I asked him the usual litany of questions while adding up his bill; Had he used the phone? Did he use parking at any time? Did he have dinner downstairs during his stay? Nope, nope, nope.
I commented that I hadn't seen him around during his stay.
"I just slept," he said grinning.
"You just slept?" I asked.
"Yes, and it was great! I had a nice room in the back, and I just stayed in there and slept for four days."
He sounded extraordinarily pleased. "It was great!"

Since I am a man who likes his sleep, I recognized the genius in that approach to any hotel stay.
"You've just become one of my favorite guests of all time," I told him.
"Really?"
"Absolutely. You understand us completely. It's the very definition of what we offer. I'm glad to meet somebody who finally understands."
Some people like their guests running around in the streets in the middle of the night without any clothes on screaming in French, I prefer mine hibernating in luxury for the duration of their stay, and thankful for the opportunity.

EMERGENCY REDEFINED

There are benefits to making myself available to this hotel seven days a week, twenty-four hours a day, with neither recognition nor thanks. After years of being jarred awake from a sound sleep for various reasons during the night; sleeping with one ear out for the house phone and one ear on the doorbell; I've developed some very effective sleep inducement techniques.

Which leads us to this story: One night, in the middle of the night, the emergency phone line in our bedroom rang and I picked it up to have a somewhat hysterical woman demand, "I must be put through to Mr. Safaris immediately."
I asked drowsily, "Is it an emergency? It's three o'clock in the morning here..." I knew because, my wife had just closed the book she was reading and turned off the light.
"YES, this IS an emergency," the female voice screeched, "His Aunt Edna just died."
I said, somewhat unsympathetically perhaps, "I think you should call back in the morning."
She whined, "This IS AN EMERGENCY!"
I said sleepily, "Please call back in the morning. It's three A.M." I hung up.

But, wondering if I'd done the right thing, I pulled myself up and sat on the edge of the bed in order to outline my somewhat foggy thinking on the matter.
"She'll still be dead in the morning," I concluded out loud.
My dear wife asked sleepily, "What was that about?"
I explained the situation.

Minutes later the emergency phone rang again and if you imagine sharp little elbows of encouragement being thrown in my direction by my sleepy but devoted wife, you understand the situation perfectly. I reached for the phone after about four or five rings, and knocked it off the hook. I fumbled around in the dark trying to find the handset for a while, in amongst the stacks of books, and when I finally recovered it, the woman had hung up. It hardly mattered, I was pretty sure my original thinking was correct; Aunt Edna would still be dead in the morning.

I'm guessing that the hotel rulebook would have had me get up, turn on a light, find the guest list, call Mr. Safaris' room and, after yanking him from a sound sleep, explain what I could to him, without getting too involved. Then the poor man would be abandoned to pace the floor for four or five hours before he could do anything about it.

During our brief discussion of the matter, I told my wife, "Let's just let the guy sleep."
She said quietly, "He might be able to book an early flight." But I think even she, who thinks more clearly than any person I have ever met on this planet, missed the point.

"IT DOESN'T MATTER" I said (employing her father's well-worn phrase, but infusing it with an irritated tone of my own, which he would never employ), "The woman's dead." I said. "She is dead. Whether Safaris rushes home on the first flight out of here in the morning or arrives three days later by coal train, she'll still be dead. This is not an emergency. An emergency is something you can take action and do something about."

But, once again I found myself sitting up on the edge of the bed wondering if I'd done the right thing. I was pretty sure I had, but equally sure I'd made a big mistake. I was going to be called in for this for sure.

"He might want to comfort his poor niece," pleaded my warm, nicely-tousled wife.

"I bet," I snorted derisively, "The slimy bastard! I've probably just done his poor niece a favor by keeping him away from her as long as possible."

I crawled back into bed. Sylvie laughed and curled up behind her grumpy old husband. It's kind of wonderful how my wife, as dignified and courteous and gentle and proper as she is, still makes accommodations for my peculiar sense of humor.

One night, in the middle of the night, about 4 AM, a cab driver rang the doorbell and, knowing it was a cabby, I answered the phone bitterly, as I always do at that hour. There is no reason on earth that I should be awakened to orchestrate the meeting of a cabbie and his fare.

"YES?" I snapped.

"I'm here to pick up a passenger."

"What's the passenger's name?"

"Caldero."

I got up and turned on a light and looked at the chart. We didn't have anyone named Caldero as a guest.

"What's the guest's room number?"

"I don't know."

"I'm afraid I can't help you then. We don't have anyone named Caldero that I know of; I need a room number."

"I don't have that."

"I can't help you then," I said, and hung up.

A couple brief moments later the door bell rang again.
"YES!"
"I'm here to pick up a passenger?"
"I need the name or the room number."
"The name is Caldero."
"We don't have anyone here by that name, and listen to me carefully please... DO NOT   RING   THAT   GOD DAMNED DOOR BELL   AGAIN!"

I went back to bed and about three minutes later (about the time it takes someone to crawl back into between the covers and get perfectly comfortable) the guy LEANED on that doorbell. He just leaned on it. It must have rung continuously for a full minute. I hopped out of bed, pulled on some clothes as quickly as I could and, picking up the baseball bat on my way out the door, ran down the hallway as fast as my bare feet could carry me, and, as I got to the front door... the cab was just pulling away.

When I told Sylvie this story the next morning—because she'd slept through all the action—I was laughing.
"I'm glad you can see the humor in it," she said.
I thought I detected a hint of pride in her tone. She may have mistakenly detected a burgeoning maturity that wasn't really there.
"My god," I said, "who couldn't see the humor in that? The guy did exactly what I would have done. Only, I would have waited in my cab long enough to lure him out into the street, in the hopes that he'd lock himself out."

INJUSTICE IS BLIND

Of course all of our regular guests are perfectly reasonable and a constant pleasure to deal with, but they don't all start out that way. Like the gentleman I spent 15 minutes talking to over the telephone answering questions about; room sizes, parking, the restaurant, the weather, and taking down all of his personal information; name, phone number, credit card numbers, arrival time and cetera, when he suddenly asked, "Do you work there?"

I laughed and said, good naturedly, "If I didn't why would I have been talking to you all this time?"

And the good gentleman snapped, "I don't need your sarcasm. I asked you, do you work there?"

"I'm not being sarcastic," I said in purest innocence. "What do you mean... ?" I thought about it. "Oh, you mean am I in San Francisco, as opposed to India or somewhere?"

"I told you once already, I don't need your sarcasm."

"I am not being sarcastic. I guess I have no idea what you mean."

"Well, I don't like your attitude at all. Don't tell me you're the manager there."

"Don't worry, I won't," I said.

"I've told you I don't need any more of your sarcasm."

He thought a bit. "Good god, don't tell me you own it."

"If I did I wouldn't be here," I said.

"WHAT is your name?"

"My name is Edward."

"Well, Edward, the woman I spoke to this afternoon was simply lovely. She was very nice and she didn't respond to every question with sarcasm. She was very nice."

"I'm sure she was. That's why I married her."

"This is absolutely atrocious! I want no more of your sarcasm. Do you hear me? I didn't call there to be treated in this manner. How can I make that any more clear?"
"Would you like to cancel this reservation?"
"No."
"Are you sure?"
"There you go again."

It went on like that for far too long as far as both of us were concerned (and I leave it to you to decide which of us was the idiot); but I stopped myself from saying what I felt needed to be said a dozen times during that conversation. What I've always felt like saying in these instances is this. "You know, you can make things as difficult as you want and I'll be glad to accommodate you. But, basically, making a reservation is a simple, civil matter which doesn't require any contention whatsoever." But, the guest makes the rules; I only play by them. If the guest wants to turn our interaction into a pitched battle of some sort, I feel obliged to make his efforts pay off. If he wants to keep things simple and direct, I'll do that too.

One of the things that you learn in the hotel business is that if you help people, they will resent it. If you show them exceptional consideration and saintly forbearance, fielding their endless questions while other guests stack up outside in the hallway with smoldering tinder under their bare soles and their saintly eyes raised in divine patience toward Heaven, the guest you're pampering will not appreciate the sacrifice you are all making. On top of that, if you simply can not give them what they want, because, for example, *it is impossible*, they will be convinced that you are being purposefully uncooperative. Give them what they ask for, but without the appropriate cowering, stuttering and drooling, and they will turn bitter before your eyes.

Somehow to put up with demanding people is to offend them further. The more you put up with, the greater the offense. It would be impossible to list all of the examples we might offer here which would demonstrate this principle at work. I confess that I could probably come up with many more stories than anyone else on staff, but I have an edge over them when it comes to offending our demanding guests—since I am the one most likely to show up at their door to handle their catastrophe.

Additionally, I'm the only one around here who doesn't have a charming foreign accent. So, my name springs immediately to mind when they try to pinpoint the reason for their discontent. And again, in this small, privately owned French hotel when such matters come to trial, the employee is always the guilty party.

Once the owner has made up his mind—and he made up his mind on this sort of thing more than thirty years ago—no amount of evidence will change it. At no time during the prosecution will things like facts or the truth be allowed in before the employee's condemnation, and ultimate public humiliation. Oh, and the guest will receive a bottle of good wine as a kind of compensation, on his way out the door. The rule is the same at most hotels, the more pretentious, the more pompous the guest, the more effusive the apology, and the finer the bottle of wine.

BEING FRANK

A woman calls down to the front desk to ask if she can get any heat in her bathroom. "It's too cold in there, and I'm afraid it'll be cold when I get out of the shower."
I explain that there is no heat in the bathroom per se, and ask her if it is too cold in her room as well.
"I'll go down and turn on the heat if it's too cold in your room, but I really don't think heat is required tonight," I explain.
"No, no-no, the room is just fine. We don't need heat in the room, but the bathroom is cold."
"I'm sorry, there's no heat in the bathroom."
"Nothing? No electric heater or anything?"
"I'm sorry, no."
She simply hangs up.

Ten minutes later she's on the phone again with the same concerns and we have basically, if not word-for-word, the very same conversation with one difference: now she is really discontent. She can't believe that there is no heat in her bathroom or that I don't care enough to begin installing it immediately, I guess by magic. So, being much more caring that anyone ever gives me credit for, I offer to come up and see if there might be some solution to her problem. She challenges me to do that.

I arrive, knock, enter when invited by this tragically abused guest. I enter the bathroom with her permission and discover that it IS cold in there. I also discover the reason for the chill. She has the window wide open. I close it, and coming from the bathroom announce, "It should get warmer in there now. The window was open; I closed it for you."

"I wanted that window open," she says in a manner a queen might use while addressing the most idiotic and irritating of her many irritating idiotic servants.

I'm at a loss. My face probably reveals it.

"It will remain cold in there as long as you have the window open." I explain. "If you close the window, it should warm up." I'm careful with the way I explain that, being particularly cautious. This situation has a nasty feel to it, and a familiarity which I want desperately to avoid.

"I want that window open for the air!" she wails.

"Well," I sigh deeply, "you can have the air or you can have the heat, but…" I didn't want to get into the basic physical laws of nature that were the foundation for my argument, and I cringed at the thought of having her explain her thinking to me.

"I wanted that window open," she wails again, "I want the air."

I look at the woman. She looks at me. Neither of us understands the other. I'm busy thinking, trying to find the solution to this dilemma, but nothing in my 62 years experience on earth, either through my formal education or gathered from reading, or conveyed to me on any drunken night by a somewhat sloshy friend, provides me with an answer to the situation.

"I don't know what I can do for you," I say calmly.

"Well, you've been MOST helpful!" she says snidely. "What's you name?"

"Frank," I say. "My name is Frank."

PEDWARD

If guests are sitting in the lobby when it's time to lock up, reading a nice book or chatting, while 14th century choral music plays in the background, I might, instead of giving them the bum's rush, offer them a glass of red wine. This does not mean that I have lost my mind completely, as the startled look on their faces may indicate. It only means that the vision, the dream, the illusion of this lovely little idyll, the aspiration and the spirit of this small, privately owned French hotel has seeped into a tiny crack in my otherwise impenetrable armor and, perhaps, produced a temporary glitch in my obstinacy. Looking closely, I worry that I may have begun to bear the patina of an evolving being.

When I do these things of course I have no doubt that the owner would approve, but I do them anyway.

My only fear is that if I do that kind of thing too frequently, someday I may emerge from our rooms chirping like a tiny little bird and fall upon the neck of each arriving guest while cooing, "Welcome, dear friend. Welcome!" as though truly pleased to see them. That's why whenever I'm nice to people I brush it off as quickly as I can, and I make them promise not to tell my boss. It doesn't work though… they never do.

On occasion we have small groups of Russians staying for a week or so at the hotel. Typically there are 8, 10 or 12 of them and we place them each in their own room, sharing a bath with one of their associates. This occurs a couple of times a year and it's a fairly routine affair; we check them in, have the interpreter explain a variety of things to them as a group, then, two by two, I escort them up in the elevator to their rooms. There I welcome them each and show them how the keys work.

My extraordinarily wonderful wife, who has been infatuated with Russian culture and history since she was a young girl; who had a Russian tutor whom she loved dearly for many years, insists that Russians are not sullen by nature. It is always amazing to me the kind of things the pure of heart choose to blind themselves to. Any casual observer of Russians suffering the crushing daily trials of life might conclude otherwise; and many have; even Russians themselves. For example, it would be difficult for any honest observer to ignore Pushkin's observation that "Heaven gives us habit in place of happiness."

An aside:
But sullenness is not the sole trait of Russians; they are also snide. One day, my dear wife and I had the use of her best friend's condo—a woman of Russian descent. And we were in the community swimming pool splashing around when I found myself falling in love with her all over again. So, I pulled her to me and gave her a long passionate kiss. Two Russian women lying around like beached whales in lawn chairs near the edge of the pool exchanged glances. One of them rolled her eyes and said something to the other in Russian. In response her friend snorted derisively, and they both laughed in a vulgar cynical manner that needed no translation. I know sarcasm when I hear it. I asked Sylvie what the woman had said, and she told me that she had said, "LOVE has come to the swimming pool!"

I lived across the hall from an ancient Russian journalist for 14 years and, through her, I met quite a few Russians. And I know them generally to remain fairly dour until they've had a few vodkas—then, come on now, admit it my friend, we are all Russians at heart.

At any rate…

Usually these groups arrive late in the evening, beaten, taciturn, hungry, travel weary, strangers in a peculiar land. They're saying little even amongst themselves as they wait sullenly, like sheep waiting to be shorn. I announce the names of two of them, pronouncing the names as best I can; show them to the elevator, show them to their rooms, show them how the keys work and run down stairs to escort the next two up to their rooms. I don't know why, sometimes I take to a particular person and make a little extra effort to welcome them. I feel compelled by unknown forces to make these select individuals understand that our hotel is their home for the next little while. I do a lot of smiling and nodding… and surprisingly, I mean it.

Usually, it is someone with a physical handicap of one sort or another; a lisp or a limp, bad breath, an embarrassing choice in headgear, a good woman married to a moronic brute, or a nice guy married to an unbearable moronic brute. On this particular occasion there was a gentleman named Posonov who appeared to have taken the trip from Russia especially hard. To my ever-caring eye he seemed to be in particular need, and what's left of my natural kindness welled up within me the minute I set eyes on him. So, I decided that I was going to shatter the language barrier using only the most basic tools of our trade, faux courtesy and a perpetually pasted-on smile.

Posonov was going to enjoy his stay at our hotel or I was going to die in the effort. In the end, Mr. Posonov would look back and recall our little hotel with fondness. "…and that guy, Edward…well, what can one say about such a wonderful warm human being?"

Right from the beginning I focused in on Mr. Posonov. I'm making special efforts to call him by name—something guests seem to all revel in, for reason which I will never understand—saying, "This is your room, Mr. Posonov. And here, Mr. Posonov… the keys, Mr. Posonov… Oh, and breakfast is served, Mr. Posonov, from 7:30 until…" But Mr. Posonov is not having it. He's tired. He doesn't understand the language too well. My consideration means nothing to him. Apparently he thinks I'm goading him. I'm sensitive. I'm caring. I'm courteous beyond expectation, and good-natured far beyond my own natural limits. And I'm getting the idea that this is only irritating him. So, I back off a little. I'm patient. These things take time.

Over the next few days, I make a point of restricting myself to, "Hello Mr. Posonov" when he goes by the office. "Good evening, Mr. Posonov" as he goes down to dinner, and, "Oh, Mr. Posonov… would you like a wake-up call?"

One day, no towels appear, as if by magic, in his room. The maids who normally perform this highly technical, extremely complicated and somewhat delicate sleight of hand have failed to follow through. Mr. Posonov calls down to ask, somewhat irritably, for towels, and I spring into action. I go dashing downstairs and get the towels and fly upstairs again with fresh towels for Mr. Posonov.

"Here you go, Mr. Posonov," I say with my very best artificial smile firmly fixed. And I realize that I am still trying to win this guy over when I find myself saying, "I assure you, Mr. Posonov, that we beat our maids as thoroughly as the finest establishments."
He looks at me for a long while.

"What is *wrong* with you?" he demands.
"Wrong with me?" I ask in complete innocence.
The blank look in my eye, the wrinkles in my forehead are both proof of my perfect innocence, but he doesn't see them, or he doesn't interpret them correctly.
"Good day, Mr. Posonov." he begins mimicking me, "Good afternoon, Mr. Posonov. Here are your towels, Mr. Posonov!" He's spitting out the words with bitter distaste.

I'm surprised of course. I don't know what to say to this. I don't know what he's getting at. I have never ever treated anyone better than I've been treating Mr. Posonov. And, as said, guests usually love that sort of pabulum.
"What is your name?" he asks.
"Edward," I tell him.
"How would you like it if I called you Pedward?"

Now, I am even more confused; I'm completely lost. But Posonov's train has already left the station, he's getting up a full head of steam, and it looks like he's not going to be satisfied until he runs the thing right off the tracks. By now it's obvious that he's talking to an idiot; the blank look in my eye, the wrinkles in my forehead are both undeniable proof of my perfectly idiotic nature. He sees them. He knows how to interpret them.

From my side of the divide I can only see the great void that lies between myself and Mr. Posonov. I have no idea how it came to this. I tried. I really did.

With nothing to say, I wait.

"My NAME is ROSonov!" he shouts, "not Posonov. ROSONOV." He takes the towels and slams the door.

Back at the office I pull his file, and sure enough, the guy's name is Rosonov. Well, so much for a pleasant little stay at our hotel. But, I think I gave him the memorable experience I'd hoped for.

The next day, the Russians checked out. As he passes the front desk, dragging his suitcase, Mr. Rosanov does not turn his head in my direction or stop to say goodbye.

One Final Note:
I thought this was a pretty good story until my wife told me that… as fate would have it… that particular group of Russians was here on a program to study *customer service.*

So, it's even a better story than I thought. And, this one doesn't even need to come to trial; I plead guilty.

LATE DEPARTURE

SCENE: A gentleman, arriving very late at night, stands before me. Since it is not unusual at all for such late arrivals to depart early on the following day (something I will never understand) I ask, "Will you be checking out early?"
"No. about noon," he says.
"Check out time is 11," I say.
"Can I have a late check out?"

I look at the chart to see if his room is slated for occupancy the following day. It is.
"I'm sorry but all our rooms are taken and the maids need to prepare that room for arriving guests," I say.
"How about 11:40?" he asks, "Because, I have an important appointment."
"What time is your appointment?"
"Noon. I really have to be there on time."
"Well," I say, "it would behoove you to check out *earlier* rather than *later* if you have an important appointment at noon, wouldn't it?" I offer this thought in an apologetic manner, because I know from experience that rational thought can be offensive to some… many… most people.
"Uh, well… yeah, I guess you're right." He mulls. "How about 11:30 then?"
"Check out time is 11. If you'd like to leave your bags with us while you go to your meeting, just bring them down when you check out."
"Oh, OK. So, I *can't* have a late check out?"
"I would give it to you if I could."
"Yeah, well, thanks for nothin'," he says flatly.

After showing him to his room I know that I have done something wrong here, but I can not, for the life of me, figure out what it is. I'm sure I'll hear about it though.

THAT WINNING LOGO

I'm not really a desk clerk, more of a night guy in desk clerk's clothing, but I try. And in my awkward attempts to be 'warm' and 'welcoming' and whatever normal desk clerks pretend to be, with greater success, I sometimes find myself wandering over the line into weirdly chatty.

My father once told me that all it took to obtain tremendous success in this country was *one good idea*… and about $80,000. I was 14 at the time and had come up with dozens of good ideas, it was the 80,000 bucks I lacked. (That was about 1963. These days the buy-in is one good idea and maybe $800,000.) One of my good ideas was, instead of a single faucet mounted on the rim of a bathtub, you place maybe six, maybe eight of the things around the edge of the side of the tub and cast those inlets at an angle. As I envisioned it, then the water would swirl around and it would create a pleasant, relaxing effect. While I was looking around under the couch cushions for the 80,000 smackers I needed to launch that idea, some guy named Jacuzzi appeared on the scene. This has happened to me more than once; I guess it has for everybody.

So, with that in mind, some kids have checked in and I'm showing them to their room on the sixth floor and as the young woman gets in the elevator I notice that she has a large word painted on the back of her sweatshirt and outlined in rhinestones. As the door to the elevator closes I say to her, "I noticed that you have something written on your back in rhinestones, but I didn't get a chance to read it. What does it say?"

186

She says, "Pink."

I say, "Pink?"

She says, "It's a brand."

"Hmm, I say," and after giving it some thought I say, "You know, when I was a kid, early 60's sometime, Dodge came out one year with the word 'DODGE' in huge block letters on the tailgate of all their trucks. Let me see what floor we're going to." I looked at the key and remembered that we had a few more floors to go. "And that year, farmers throughout the Midwest boycotted Dodge. They REFUSED to buy any of those trucks. The consensus seems to be, "I am NOT driving around advertising for Dodge!" It was looking pretty bad for Dodge... until the next year, when suddenly ALL of the manufacturers came out with their names emblazoned on their tailgates." I turned around to look into the blank faces of our arriving guests.

"You know," I said, continuing just as though they might be the audience such insight deserves, "There was this kid in Encinitas, surfer kid, when I lived down there. And his name was Rusty. And he put his initial, a big sloppy kind of 'R' on a couple t-shirts and asked all his surfer buddies to wear them on the beach. Before long... Oh here's we are on the sixth floor. Six-Oh-Six is this way... Before long he also had them wearing shorts with his initial on 'em, and in a couple very short years he had an entire surfer-kid clothing line that consisted of nothing more than a bunch of stuff with his initial on it. I think today that kid's some kind of a millionaire."

I opened the door to their room, turned on the light, went in and placed their bag on the bench. I told them how the overhead fan and light worked, and explained the two key system to them before saying, "The reason I tell you this is that, instead of walking around advertising for Pink, you should put *your name* on the back of some sweatpants and ask all your friends to walk around in them for a while… see if anything good breaks off and falls your way."

Apparently there was nothing anyone could say in response to that. I waited an appropriate time before I stepped back out into the hall. And, as I pulled their door shut I glance in and saw those kids looking at each other like, "What the hell was that stupid old bastard yammering about?"

They're right of course. In my attempts to be friendly, I often fly pretty close to the sun. One time I was downstairs and had my foot on the bottom step, about to come up, when a man descended quickly, almost knocking me down. "I'm sorry," he said, "but I have to pee really badly." "That's OK, do the best you can," I quipped. My thinking was, 'The guy's almost as old as I am, he oughta be able to pee with reasonable skill by now. His thinking was, 'What…?' Or, at least that was the look he gave me.

The guest was right. Arbitrarily thoughts plucked from some distant universe, oblique references to pop tunes, and business advice are not what guests really expect when in communication with the hotel staff.

'Just another reason I should be hung, I guess.

WATER EVERYWHERE and A BLIND MAN CHECKING IN

From experience I can tell you two things. The first is that when a guest says something is an emergency it rarely is, and the second is that when it comes to overflowing toilets, the remedy can take twenty minutes or thirty minutes or forty minutes, any single one of which may seem like a befouled eternity. Actually there is a corollary to that: when it is an actual emergency involving an overflowing tub or toilet, the guests are often completely unaware of it, and are startled when I come pounding upon their door to tell them water's coming through the ceiling of the room below.

So that is why I chose to continue to check in the blind gentleman and his wife, instead of rushing to 208. Contrary to the lady's accusation that I'd said, "I'll get there when I get around to it.", I had actually said, "I will be there as soon as I possibly can.", and I called down to the restaurant to ask them to send the dishwasher to 208 in the meantime.

I had the option, naturally, of asking the blind gentleman and his very pleasant wife—who were seated before me, in the midst of the check-in process—to sit out in the lobby and wait until I came back, not knowing how long that would be. I chose instead to finish checking them in. Then I put them on the elevator and wished them luck, while I went directly to the room where the bathroom was flooding. It was the wrong thing to do of course. But, whatever I would have done, would have been the wrong thing to do. Of that I am certain.

That was confirmed when I returned and found the owner standing outside the office talking with some arriving guests. He thought it would be fun, in an authoritative sort of way, to humiliate me by reprimanding me in front of them, for abandoning my post.

"Where have you been?" he whined. "Your most important task is to be in this office so you can welcome our guests."

"Actually," I said, "my most important task was to stop the flooding in room 208."

The look he gave me assured me that, although I might not be found guilty for preventing a serious plumbing problem, I was still guilty of not being in two places at once.

ANOTHER PLANET

We live in a world in which many people seem to be looking for every opportunity to be offended, and that's kind of a pain in the neck for those us of struggling to cling to a positive view of humanity. Why would you assume someone you're dealing with has bad intentions toward you? Why would you turn something clever into an insult, instead of accepting it in the good-natured way it was offered? What way is that to live? I'm supposedly some kind of a despicable old curmudgeon, and I don't even live like that. With that in place, you're now prepared for this.

Some kids were checking in from Switzerland and, after I offered them a seat, I sat down and said, "Right on time!" The male of the couple said, "What?" The female looked a bit confused. So, I explained that Switzerland has a bit of a reputation for precision, especially in matters concerning time. The male said, just a slight bit peevishly I thought, "Well, we are glad to be able to fulfill your stereotype of the Swiss people." He did a pretty good imitation of glaring at me, but I could see right through that and detected a beating heart within.

I smiled and said, "Well, it could be worse. A couple of weeks ago I had a little matter of difference with one of the guests over the phone, and when she came down to confront me face to face she walked in and declared, "I should have know it would be some old white bastard with a tie."
They both laughed heartily.

"You're right," said the male, "being known for promptness is perhaps not so bad after all."
Because of this I now know that the Swiss are a people, though harboring an overly-fine sensitivity when it comes to matters of stereotypical exactitude, quick to forgive. Such forgiveness is no longer the case in the U.S. however.

Our entire culture was built, and fairly solidly too, upon our continual ribbing of each other. Unfortunately, those days are now gone; these days everyone's a victim, and too often it becomes a matter for lawyers and legislation.

A gentleman comes down to the lobby to use the computer which we have there for our guests, and it doesn't seem to be working for him. He comes to me saying, "I can't seem to make this computer work, what can I do?"
I say jovially, "I don't know what any of us can do…maybe you could move to another planet." Assuming the man of reasonable intelligence and of reasonable good nature, I'm suggesting—though perhaps somewhat obliquely—that we're all stuck with runaway technology and that there is little hope of freeing ourselves of it, on this planet. I get up and follow him into the lobby, and bend over the computer and struggle with the thing myself for about ten minutes, until I get him up and running. Remember that fact.

After a while he's in the office doorway again. He says, "I know that you don't care, you obviously couldn't care less, but that computer doesn't work. I can't get it to do anything. All I wanted to do was to look up directions to see where we were going and I can't get it to work; it's so slow and full of stuff…"

I interrupt him to say, "Where is it you'd like to go?"
I'm prepared to help him using the office computer.
He cuts me off. "NO. You already made it perfectly clear to
me that you don't care."
I'm startled. I must look it. I have no idea what he is talking
about, and I tell him as much.
"You told me to move to another planet and, clearly, I'm
interrupting you... Just never mind. I'll go back to my
room now and remain silent." He walks out of the office
and over to the elevator and pushes the button.

I follow him saying, "Wait, you're misunderstanding what I
said. It wasn't about you; I was talking about our
dependence on computers."
He says, "I'm not listening to you any more. I don't need
your sarcasm. I ask for your help and you tell me to move
to another planet." He pushes the button.
"I wasn't saying anything about you," I say as the elevator
door closes and the thing begins to lift. "I was speaking
about the situation we're *all* in!" I shout as the thing
disappears. Is anybody with me on this?

This is almost custom-made to cause me trouble.
Forget the fact that I tried to help him. Forget the fact that I
offered to look-up whatever he needed on our computer.

The man asks for my help and I tell him, "Hey, why don't
YEW move to another planet. I don't got no time for dis
right now!" That's the way it'll be told, and that the way
the owner will hear it. Let's just call it another example of
my brutal and completely-uncalled-for mistreatment of our
guests. It'd be useless for me to attempt to explain it.

I continually make the same mistake: assuming all of our guests are intelligent and good natured.

I also continually forget that they don't assume the same about me.

For this, I should be hung. I admit it. It would certainly make things easier for me.

LOST RESERVATION

There are occasional heartbreaking times when good
guests, nice people, kind people, gentle unassuming people,
whom anyone would take an immediately liking to and
only wish to see happy, check in, and from the moment
they set foot in the door until the taxi I've ordered to take
them back to the airport doesn't show up on time, they are
hounded by one tiny disaster after another. It begins when I
lift their luggage and the handle breaks.

We get to their room and the maids have left the window
open. It's too cold in there; they are old folks and they want
their room to be warm. It's summer, I can't turn on the
heat; when the heat is on, all the rooms are heated;
everyone in the place would suffer. I struggle to explain
this to them but only come across as an uncooperative,
unkind, and uncaring brute.
Then their toilet plugs up.
The maids have forgotten to leave them towels.
It's just the beginning.

When they go down to breakfast they arrive late and the
place is closed. In the evening, the restaurant—which
they've heard so much about and have looked forward to
trying—is closed for a private party. They ask me for a
recommendation for dinner and the two places I can
honestly recommend, are too far away for them.

Throughout all of this I look bad. I've been able to give
them nothing they've asked for, not even heat.

When this kind of thing happens, every effort to turn things around for these good people either fails or makes things worse. Irony at it's most ironic. It is as if Fate has conspired to give them a bad time, and I have been chosen the instrument of their torture.

But, most of the people who have a bad stay here are just miserable people doing what they must to maintain and nurture the smoldering discontent in their lives.

Suddenly a woman stands before me in the doorway to the office. She doesn't look like a nice person. I can handle that because, by all accounts, excluding those issued by my loving wife, I don't look like a nice person either.
"What can I do for you?" I say in a professional manner.
"We have a reservation. We'd like to check in," she says snappishly. And you know, it is far too soon in the proceedings to be getting snappish, but at least now I know what kind of cards she holds.
"Come in," I say with reserve, "You're welcome to have a seat."
As I say this I can already hear the owner's voice bemoaning my handling of the situation. "No smile; no greeting... Can you not offer this nice lady a proper greeting?"
In his world this person would be considered a *nice lady*.
"Please," I say with kindness, "have a seat."
"I'd rather stand," she says as if offended. Her husband, balding and meek, prefers to stand as well; he stands in silence out in the hallway, as she handles the transaction.
"As you wish. What is the name?" My tone is only slightly challenging.

196

"Thornsby."

I look through the files of arriving guests and there is no Thornsby. "I'm sorry," I say, "but we're not expecting anyone with the name of Thornsby, could the reservation have been made under another name?"

"Oh GREAT, Edmond, they've LOST our reservation!" she wails to her husband. The gentleman rolls his eyes and sighs the sigh of a good man stuck in a bad situation until, by God's great mercy, death does them, at long last, part.

"Could the reservation have been made under another name?" I urge.

"Well, Newcomb then." I notice that her snappishness has not diminished.

I look through the files again, this time being careful to check for both a Thornsby, which I might have overlooked the first time, as well as Newcomb or any similar name. There is nothing.

"I'm sorry," I say.

"It's either Thornsby or Newcomb," she insists.

"Could it be under another name?" I've been in this business long enough to know that, though I have but a single last name, many many people have at least three, and it is those with so many last names which are ALWAYS the ones who...

"Spindleworth," she snaps with venom.

It's now my fault that she can't keep track of her names. I go through the files yet again; this time I am looking for Thornsby, Newcomb, Spindleworth or anything that might be similar.

"I'm sorry," I say, and I truly am. But, I look beyond her to poor Edmond and I am even sorrier for him.

I take a brief moment to thank God that I am who I am and not that poor man. My guess is that if I were, I'd also be in prison.

"Well, do you, by chance have anything under Dankleton?" She's livid.
I don't need to look through the files this time—not because by now I have memorized the names and room numbers of every incoming guest, though I had—but because it has been the top file throughout this entire ordeal (and I think ordeal describes it).

I am tempted—but only very slightly—to inquire how this tall, pale and eternally brittle, middle-aged woman has managed to accumulate so many last names, but I have an inkling. I glance beyond her and I can see that poor old Edmond is one of those dear, honest, kind, simple, soft-spoken and, given the chance that he will never be given, entertaining men who has, by the wear and tear of married life, been forced to place one foot in his own coffin and looks forward, with resigned hope, to that moment when he might be finally nudged to step in entirely.

As I always do in this situation—for this woman is not unique but merely a type which would be readily recognized by anyone in the "hospitality industry"—I reissued my little prayer of thanks while taking them up to the room, which I know will not be to her liking.

Throughout the very long and cold ride up in the elevator I am aware that I have deeply offended this woman, though I can not, for the life of me, determine precisely how.

I am also aware that this woman will, during her stay find no less than a dozen, a thousand, a million things wrong with our little establishment; things not up to her standard; service unacceptable; our response to her endless questions not to her liking, and the lower the staff bows the more displeased she'll become. That too is predictable.

And it'll all be my fault.

THE CASUAL OBSERVATIONS OF A PHONE ANSWERER

Some of our guests are the most popular people on earth. That is the only conclusion one can possibly draw from the number of phone calls they receive. Sometimes the pace of incoming phone calls to a particular room is so frantic that the callers stack up like planes above Dallas/Fort Worth. There is a tone of desperation in their voices as they ask for room #303. What leads to such popularity I can not guess. When my wife and I are in a hotel there are no calls in and typically only two calls out, if that many.

I do not envy these guests whose phone never stops ringing, I do not sympathize, but I do wonder about them. When, for example, do they use the bathroom, or eat or get any sleep? When do they read or play the cello? All I have to do to generate an incoming call is to put my feet up and begin to feel the slowly spreading comfort of relaxation. So I wonder what these guests are up to which initiates so many incoming calls. Perhaps they're meditating.

Some of our guests have very short attention spans. That is the conclusion I draw from the fact that someone of their acquaintance will call, ask to be put through to them, and speak to them for 30 seconds, and then, less than five minutes later, will call again, ask to be put through to them again and then, less than five minutes later, will call and ask to be put through to them again, and then, less than five minutes later, will call and ask to be put through to them again, and then, less than five minutes later, will call and ask to be put through to them again.

This will go on as long as that person is a guest here; every afternoon, every evening, until they depart… or until I go insane, whichever comes first.

This is not unusual behavior. And although it does not happen with all of our guests, or even most or our guests, it happens with enough of our guests to make me wonder about it, to make me think about it. I have pondered it, and I have gnawed on it, and I have given it my very best imitation of thought, and I must admit that I have absolutely NO idea what is going on there.

I have absolutely NO idea why that person who calls—and in most cases it seems to be the same person each time—doesn't simply say everything that he has to say in a single call, with maybe a secondary call to accommodate afterthought. But, they don't. That's the way it is. It's like a French goodbye.

First there is the preparation to say goodbye, then there is the preliminary goodbye followed by what appears to be a goodbye but isn't. That is followed by a lot of chatter and kissing and shaking of hands and telling of brief but entertaining tales, before a tentative goodbye is issued. Then they break off into groups, males with males, females with females. Then there is the hugging and a step is made toward the door; goodbyes are then said all around. The door is opened and held in that position as goodbyes are once again exuded in a most sincere and meaningful manner; there is some quiet laughter involved. The guests then step through the doorway and the door closes behind both those who must depart and those who must regrettably remain behind, but who now find themselves also drawn outside. There is some discussion upon the sidewalk for a period of time, usually involving politics or education. There is more laughter. Someone recites a fragment of poetry. There is joviality, and many thanks, and some *not at all* and some *yes, it was quite nice wasn't it?* and goodbyes are exchanged in a tentative manner. Then there is the kissing and shaking of hands again and those who must leave do so but turn to wave sadly (but with hope!) every 14 paces, and those who must regretfully remain behind weep openly (with tears of joy, no doubt) while waving and making efforts to still their frantically beating hearts. After all, they have not seen these wonderful people since last week and it will be three of four more days before they see them again.

My wife was left completely in shock the first time my parents said goodbye and then simply walked out the door. "Were they angry with me?' she asked with great concern. "No. Why?"
"Because they said good night and…well…then…" she could not go on. I'm not sure she entirely understood it.

Perhaps this is what those phone calls are like; perhaps they are something like a French goodbye.
"Hello, Evelyn, how are you?"
"Just fine."
"When did you get in?"
"We just arrived."
"Well, OK. I'll call you back again in six seconds."
"Oh, that'll be just dandy!"
"Well, goodbye then."

"Goodbye. And try not to call me back so soon that we haven't yet finished one conversation before we must launch out upon another."

"Yes, I've noticed that that can sometimes happen. But, usually, in order to prevent that, I count to four before pressing redial."

"Oh, how clever! I should try that myself."

"Well, goodbye then. Speak to you soon."

"Not soon enough though."

"Well, I seem to be dawdling. I'll hang up now and call you right back."

"I can hardly wait."

LORD of the FLIES

Although this guest was not helpless, demanding, rude, unbearable, or insane, he was at once somehow all of that.

Harrrold Gorrrdon rrrolled in rrrolling his rrrrs and calling me by my first name the day he arrived. For several years after that, he came frequently and stayed for weeks at a time. He was a demanding sort of fellow, and he very much enjoyed talking down to me. What bothered me about this was that he assumed I enjoyed it as well. The gentleman was under the impression that he was, if not the sole tenant in this small, privately owned French hotel, then certainly its most imporrrrtant.

His requests broke down into two categories; *Edwarrrrd, can y' brrring me…?*
"Edwarrrrd, can y' brrring me some extrrrra pilluhs?"
"Edwarrrrd, can y' brrrrring me anotherrrr iron. I dun't like the looks o' this one."
"Edwarrrrd, can y' brrrrring me a couple o' frrresh towels? These could have used a betterrrr cleanin'."

…and, *Edwarrrrd, is it normal?*
"Edwarrrrd, is it normal to have such a terrrrible picture on this herrrre television?"
"Edwarrrrd, is it normal to hearrr every bit o' the trrraffic as it goes by muh window?"
"Edwarrrrd, is it normal to have it so very hot in this rrrrroom?"
He always expected an immediate response. If not, the next phone call I received was from Mr. Gordon again.

"Edwarrrrd, arrre y' plannin' on doin' somethin' about the…?"

Mr. Gordon was something of a ladies' man. Whenever he passed by the office with a new or different woman on his arm he would slow his pace so that I could get a good look at her. They were all pretty much of a type: reasonably attractive, slightly worn but stately, middle-aged blondes. "I won't be needin' a wake-up call tomorrrrow, Edwarrrd," he'd say with a click of his tongue, a nod of his head, and a wink of one clever eye.

These are the words of a lord speaking to his favorite, most devoted underling. It was a ploy, because he never asked for a wake-up call any other time either. It does not pay to gawk, especially when that's what's expected of you, and it does no good to raise your eyebrows or scratch your head or try to see the reason in it all, but, Mr. Gordon, who was to me hardly more than a periodic throbbing pain, was, to the ladies, what he himself called, *worrrrth knowin'*. (wink)

Every time he checked out Mr. Gordon told me how he felt about the hotel, about us, about the service. Basically, he di-nuh rrrreally like this hotel and he di-nuh know why he continued to come herrrre. The place was just terrrrible. Therrre arrre neverrr enough pilluhs, and the rrrroom is always too darrrrrn hot. But he came back anyway.

One day, shortly after he arrived, he called down to ask, "Edwarrrrd, is it normal to have all these flies in here?"
"Flies?" I asked.

"There arrr hundreds of 'em in heerrrre, Edwarrrrd.
They're swarrrmin' all overrr."
"Flies?"
"Come up and see forrr yourrrself, Edwarrrd."

Now, I have been in this business for a while and I know
that when a guest says 'hundreds of flies' it means two, or
maybe three; there's a slight possibly that it may mean as
many as four. In their own home a thousand flies would be
called a few; in the hotel business a single gnat can become
a lawsuit. So, I went up… and indeed there were dozens of
flies in the man's room. Dozens hell, there were hundreds
of 'em. I was astonished by this because the people who
had stayed in that room the night before mentioned no flies;
the maids who cleaned that room before Mr. Gordon's
arrival mentioned no flies; when I went up to place the
seven extra pillows M. Gordon always required before his
arrival, there were no flies. Now, I could not deny it, the
place was swarrrmin' with flies. There werrr hundrrreds of
'em in theerrrre.

"So, what are y' plannin' to do about this, Edwarrrd?" he
said standing in the middle of the room and swatting wildly
at the things as they flew by.

I was almost too stunned to speak. I'd never seen such a
thing before and I didn't really know what to do. We did
have a rusty old can of flying insect spray around
somewhere—because once there was a fly in the men's
room downstairs—but I didn't want to spray poison in
there with him present. And Mr. Gordon was here for such
a long stay that I couldn't move him easily to another room.

I asked him if he would like to move but he refused—301 was "his" room; it was the room he wanted; it was the room he always stayed in.

"It's m' rrrroom, Edwarrrd; it's where I stay when I'm herrrre. Whatta you gonna do forrrr me?"

So, I ran down the block to the drug store and bought one of those god-awful things you see in old movies but with any luck you never see in real life—a hanging spiral of sticky ugly brown waxen paper ribbon—and I hung it from the center of his room, with my most sincere apologies. I mean every word of that. The presence of that THING hanging from the otherwise lovely light fixture in the center of that otherwise lovely room was embarrassing to me. But, I didn't know what else to do.

When I told Sylvie about the flies, she was surprised too, but concluded, "He must have brought them with him." I laughed at the idea but could see no other explanation. So, the next day, all the flies were gone and soon Mr. Gordon was gone. And this time, when he checked out, he told me how terrrrible the place had become and he was sure he'd neverrrr set foot in herrrrre again. And, to his credit. it was a very long time indeed before he returned.

When he did finally return, shortly after checking in, I got the call.

"Edwarrrrd, this rrrroom is swarrrrrmin' with flies again!"

"Flies? Again?"

"Did y' not hearrr me, Edwarrrd? There arrr hundreds of 'em in heerrrre. I thought you'd planned on doin' somethin' about 'em."

207

This time I could move him to another room and I did, despite his protests. I sprayed the place down thoroughly and asked the maids to wash everything in sight and closed the room down for a few days. When I told Sylvie about this second set of flies, she was even more convinced that Harrrrold Gorrrdon had brought them with him.

Is there such a thing as a maggot salesman?

When Mr. Gordon left that time, it was the last we ever saw of him… and his flies… though of course we would welcome him back any time.

"It's always a pleasure to see you again, Mr. Gorrrrdon."

CARNELLO

One Sunday night, Mr. Carnello locked his wallet, passport, plane tickets, and other miscellaneous valuables, in his room safe and lost the key. Somehow, in his mind, that was our fault. So, he didn't like this hotel—he told us as much a dozen times in half as many minutes—and swore that he'd never set foot in it again. He ranted about how lousy the place was up until the very moment he went storming out the front door. It had been quite a show, involving a reddened face, grotesque expressions, sputtering, finger-pointing, and the stomping of feet. It was like a twelve year-old girl, trapped in a fifty-six year-old man's body, trying to get out.

The key he'd lost was the only key in the world to that safe. But, muddling his argument somewhat, for those of us who remained rational during his tirade, was the fact that he'd been warned about the possibility. When I handed him the key to that safe I said (as I always do), "THIS is the ONLY key in the world to that safe, so don't lose it. The agreement is that, if you lose the key, you pay for the locksmith." As I recall, when I told him that, he responded, "Yeah, yeah, I've stayed here before; just give me the key." Complicating things just a little bit further, he discovered that he'd lost that key ten minutes before his taxi was slated to arrive and whisk him off to the airport.

So, when he showed up in the office, not just slightly but completely hysterical, screaming at me about his plight, I was forced to remind him—although I was sure he was already well aware of the fact—that the key he'd lost was the only key to that safe.

However, I did not remind him of, "Yeah, yeah, I've stayed here before; just give me the key." I wanted to help the poor man, not push him over the brink.
"I really don't know what I can do…" I pondered out loud.
"Well you gotta do somethin'" he screamed.
"Yes, I know," I said.
"I gotta get to the airport!"
"Yes, I know that too," I said. "Have you looked everywhere?"
"Yes, I've LOOKED everywhere, what do you think I've been doing?"
"Where did you keep it?"
"I kept it right here in my pocket."
"I know this sounds stupid, but would you mind checking your pocket again?" I said as meekly as a man can say such a thing.

He went into a frantic mime of some sort patting his many pockets with bulging eyes and escalating fury.
"It's not here, I tell you. YOU have to do something. What kind of a place are you running anyway? KEYS! Nobody uses keys anymore. I will never stay in this lousy hotel again. YOU gotta do something and you gotta do it NOW!"
"Yes, I know," I said and grabbed a screw driver, a hammer and about a dozen safe locks in the hope that, by chance, or through God's sweet grace, one of the other keys would open that lock.

I took the stairs three at a time, with Mr. Carnello right behind me chattering continually about keys and the airport and his wallet and that safe and what a lousy place this was and how I had to do something.

When we got to his room, I tried to force the safe open for several minutes.

"Can't you try to get that screwdriver in under that lip?"

"It's a *safe,* Mr. Carnello; it's designed to be difficult."

"Well, can't you try to pry that lock out of there?"

"It's a SAFE."

"Well, you gotta do something and you gotta do it quick."

"Yes, I'm trying to help you."

'Well what the hell kind of a place are you running here anyway? Nobody ever uses keys any more."

After force failed, I tried every one of the other safe keys and none of them would work. So, I ran back downstairs and loaded a box up with the remaining safe locks and keys and ran back up to his room and systematically tried every one of those keys, but to no avail. All of the while Mr. Carnello was bent over behind me chanting in my ear.

"You gotta do something."

"I'm trying."

"You gotta open that safe."

"Yes, that is what I'm attempting to do here."

Finally, I stood up and said, "I'll go call a locksmith."

"How long do you think that'll take?"

"I have no idea, it's hard to even get one sometimes…I'll go down and call one right away."

So, I'm in the office trying to convince the third or fourth locksmith I've talked to that, as a locksmith, he might want to do a little lock-smithing, when Mr. Carnello comes by. He tosses the keys to his room on the desk, tells me what a lousy place this is, how nobody ever uses keys any more, and how he'll never *ever* set foot in this dive again.

I'm reasonably startled. I sit up. I say, "What happened? What are you going to do?"

He says with tremendous vitriol, "I found the key."

"You found the key?"

"Yes, no thanks to you."

"Where was it?"

"In my pocket."

"In your pocket?"

He indicates the front pocket of his jacket.

"The key was in your..." I start to say.

"What I want to know is what kind of a lousy dive are you running here? Nobody uses KEYS anymore. This is the worse hotel I've ever stayed in, and I will NEVER EVER set foot in this lousy hotel again. NEVER! Goodbye."

Then Mr. Carnello goes storming out the front door.

About two months later, a man walks in one evening, sits down across from me, and says, "I have a reservation." Without comment, I go through the stack and pull Mr. Carnello's file. I hand it to him and ask him to sign at the bottom. He seems genuinely surprised by this.

"Oh, you remember me?" he says.

I say nothing. I do not shake my head. I do not snort. I do not horse-laugh.

I do not offer him a safe key either.

And he doesn't ask for one.

BILEMANN

Any small, privately owned establishment has hangers-on.
I am not speaking about returning guests—our returning
guests are our life's blood and, as far as I can see, our true
friends. I am talking about hangers-on. The owners, out of
their very good nature and their extreme generosity, have
accumulated a long list of such people, and many of them
stay here—if not for free—then for whatever price they
may have paid when they first showed up on our doorstep,
no matter how long ago that may have been. Some of our
hangers-on pay prices from the 1960's; as said, many pay
nothing whatsoever. But, whether they pay little or they
pay nothing, they all act as though they own the place.

The mystery for me is what all these fine people could have
done to deserve this life-long special consideration. That, of
course, is not my business... still I'm curious. In my
opinion, whatever it was, the debt has been repaid many
times over. Some of these people say the hotel is like their
second home, and treat it as such. When a guy checks in
and pays $60 for a room that everyone else is paying $160
for, it bugs me. It bugs me especially, if that same guy
expects us to treat him with special consideration, as if the
drastically reduced rate isn't enough.

Mr. Bilemann was one of those guests who had performed
some unknown favor for the owners in the lingering
longtime past and who, because of that favor, paid almost
nothing for his room, and would, by unspoken decree, pay
that same figure until the end of time. Bilemann was not a
stupid man. At some point he sat down, did the calculations

and determined that it was more expensive for him to stay at home than it would be to fly up here and stay at the hotel for prolonged periods; and that is what he did. And he did it regularly. But, Mr. Bilemann could not understand why his almost continual presence here did not also entitle him to more say in the way things were run.

In the beginning, when I had just moved from night guy to desk guy, Mr. Bilemann came into the office, sat down as if he owned the place, and began to delineate the many ways things around here could be improved. I didn't know what to make of that, but, when he started complaining about how unbearably hot it was in the office, I began to like the man. He could not understand why it was always so hot in this building; I too could not understand why it was always so hot in this building. He could not understand why there were three light switches in his bathroom and only one of them—the hidden one—worked. I could not understand that either. He didn't understand this, I didn't understand this; he didn't understand that, I didn't understand that. The list was endless, and we were in agreement on almost every point. We were soon to be fast friends, though I didn't particularly like the man, and I had the distinct feeling he didn't care whether I liked him or not; he had things to say and I was a stuck in that office anyway.

I recall several evenings, there at the beginning, discussing international politics with him—something I know absolutely nothing about, but like everybody else in the world, about which I have no qualms pontificating. Mr. Bilemann would start out calmly enough, recognizing the futility of it all, sitting with wrinkled brow and an occasional gesture involving upturned palms and raised shoulders, but he would soon be up on his feet pacing around and slamming his fists down on my desk, as is appropriate for such discussions… and, worst of all, I found that I agreed with the man completely... not that I give a damn. I liked what he had to say though; it all made good sense to me. There was no doubt about it, if Bilemann and I ran the world it would be a better place.

This has happened to me before—I find myself nodding my head in total agreement with someone who, in my heart of hearts, I know should probably turn my stomach. That people who are a complete embarrassment to the human race should make such sense to me on vital matters causes me some concern, of course. That's as far as my thinking goes on the matter however. When it comes to matters political I agree with people I would never want to have lunch with.

Unfortunately, it very soon became big toe/sledgehammer clear that Mr. Bilemann could not make it past the office door ever, not one time, passing in either direction, without stopping in for a very long little chat, and everything he said began to sound like a complaint. So, I began to crawl slowly toward the back of the Bilemann band wagon, looking for a place to jump off. Desk clerks are, after all, a captive audience, and, unfortunately, guests who need such an audience always sense our contractual vulnerability, and take full advantage of it. Please, if you take only one thing away with you from this book, let it be this. To engage some poor desk clerk in lengthy, near-endless, nagging conversation, no matter the subject, is wrong.

At some point during every evening Bilemann insinuated himself and opened up the chatter box with all stops out. Vox Humana eterna. Oh my God the wailing that came from that man! On a good night, a saintly night, I was entertained for three to seven minutes, and could bear nine. After that, my highly exaggerated yawning, the rolling of my eyes, the tapping of my fingers, and jumping on the phone before the first ring was truly under way, all sent no message to the man. Once he was rolling there was no stopping the man's bounding brain.

If it wasn't international politics (which grows tiresome more quickly than almost any other topic on earth), it was complaints about the hotel (which, after you've heard 'em all a dozen times, grows tiresome more quickly than international politics). Why couldn't he have the same room he had last time? Why couldn't we move the person in that room so that he could have it? Why couldn't he have the TV from that room—he liked that TV—why couldn't that TV be moved to the room he was in now? (I actually did move that TV into his new room for him one time.)

And, you know, he still didn't understand why he couldn't just have the same room every time. He'd been coming here for a very long time and he wanted to be treated like someone who had been coming here for a very long time. That was his view. Our view was he'd been coming here for a very long time and complaining about everything for a very long time and we had been tired of hearing his voice, for a very long time. In fact, in defense of the staff, we all struggled heroically against the welling urge to treat Bilemann in the manner his behavior engendered.

One evening he sat down across from me and said, "Sometimes I feel like you're the only friend I've got around here, Edward." So my attempts to escape by climbing up the wall, or slipping quietly under the desk, or placing a loaded gun in my mouth whenever he entered the office door had failed to send a clear message. Eventually everybody on staff agreed that it would be a better, finer, brighter and lovelier world, almost in every way, if Mr. Bilemann would simply go away… and by some miracle, eventually, he did.

Only after the fact was I told that the owner had stepped in.

I could hardly believe that, but it proved to be true. One day, the owner had invited the man into his office and simply asked him to go. Of course (of course, of course, of course) he worded it nicely. NICELY. The request was framed in a manner which would not offend the man or generate any hard feelings. Hemming and hawing is an important part of the small, privately-owned hotel business. So, it was an excruciating ninety minute long, face-to-face process which required finesse, long meandering sentences of nebulous meaning, and extended spells of silence, during which either party might sigh and shift uncomfortably in his chair for a while. And, as the owner himself might say, "It was not easy." In essence it boiled down to this: Look, if you don't like it here, why don't you simply go somewhere else? Which is what I would have said many years earlier, and would have taken considerable heat for saying.

And it worked. Soon, Bilemann was gone and we were left with only a weird and a somewhat sketchy memory of his views on international politics and a couple of large ratty, over-stuffed suitcases which he never returned to pick up.

I'm sure there's a lesson in there somewhere, but, if it doesn't involve martyrdom all around, I don't know what it could possibly be.

THE SHEETS

Our sheets are too short. That's what I've discovered. I
don't know why our sheets are too short, but I know that
they are. We order them from a company, whose sole
purpose is dealing in hotel sheets, and the lengths of
mattresses in the United States are pretty much
standardized; nonetheless, our sheets are too short.

While passing by the office on their way out, a young
woman stops to say somewhat peevishly, "Can you send
someone up to make our bed? There's a stain on the sheet
and it's just disgusting. Also, there are only two flat sheets.
That bed really requires a fitted bottom. I've never stayed
in a hotel where there wasn't a fitted bottom before. It
really should have a fitted bottom."
I respond by saying, "Well, I don't know much about
making beds, but I'll do what I can for you." And, she,
nose properly elevated, departs. The idea that I will take
care of the problem has somehow offended her.

When I completed whatever it was I was doing—nothing as
important as changing those sheets of course, but perhaps
having something else to do with the business of running
this hotel—I went to the linen room and poked around and
just generally made a mess of things, and discovered,
through that process, that we have only one type of sheet.
We have no fitted bottoms. I look again, this time very
carefully. We have only flat sheets; no fitted bottom sheets.
So, I take two sheets and I go up to the room and I
dismantle the bedding, folding down all the top stuff
carefully and placing it aside, and I take off the two sheets.

One of them, I note, has the kind of dim, pale ochre colored spot that is sometimes seen on our sheets and tablecloths when they come back to us freshly laundered from the linen service. The stain is the size of Akron, Ohio as it might be represented on a 12 inch globe, as seen from atop a 12-foot ladder, without glasses. It's inoffensive, it's insignificant, it's nothing icky, it's an inset, washed out, virtually non-existent, slight discoloration spanning three threads of warp and four threads weft, But the young snip has paid for clean sheets and I'm glad to give them to her.

I crumple those old sheets up and I take them out into the hall and I dump them down the laundry chute. Then, as best I can, for I am not a maid and I am not a magician, I carefully make the bed, paying particular attention to the tightness of the sheets. It is during this making of the bed that I reflect once again upon the size of our sheets. You can do whatever you will with the sides, but either at the top of the mattress or at the bottom you will come up short. There is no more than a few scant inches beyond the length of the mattress. So, I decided to sacrifice the bottom edge, and covered the top generously.

I then reassembled that bed, and I looked the room over. I then went back over and turned on the little side table lamp—thinking, that'll be nicer to come home to than the overhead light—and I left that room.

Three weeks later, this is how long she gnawed on it, the woman has written a complaint on one of those websites where the most satisfied customers limit their descriptions to 17 words, but the dissatisfied produce entire novels declaring their outrage. Once again I am the center of the complaint. It seems that I said, "I don't know anything about it, *as if (I) really couldn't care less*." The part where I said, 'but, I'll do what I can for you." has somehow been forgotten, as well as the fact that I did. There is no mention of me turning on the little side table light. According to the web-post I didn't change the sheets at all; I just turned the befouled sheet around so that the 'icky stain' was now at the foot of the bed. This is a lie. I did exactly what I just told you.

The owner, seeing this complaint on the website, prints it out and underlines the part where I say, "I don't know anything about it," *as if (I) really couldn't care less.* No questions asked, I'm guilty.

Now, about such web postings, let me speak.

To anyone on earth, ANYONE on this planet, the comments of the sane and the comments of the insane, on such sites, are quickly separated, and most readily by their size alone. The sane rarely go on and on and on about what a great time they had, delving into detail, quoting the staff and naming names. So, if the posting has more than, say, 32,000 words, it can easily be supposed, and rightly too, that it is the ranting of, if not an insane person, at least someone of questionable stability. No hotel stay, no matter how horrendous, should have such long-term impact upon any reasonable person; they just have other things to do with their brief time here on earth. But the owner can not see that. Everyone else on this planet can see that; the owner can not.

All he can see is that once again I have offended our
guests, this time by making their bed for them. The turning
on of the little table lamp would have been only more
egregious, had it somehow gotten out.
But I've done worse.

Once I offended a young couple by offering to do whatever
might be necessary should their little baby require
anything. After taking them to their room I said, "If you
need anything special for your child, let us know, and we'll
be glad to do what we can."

That was the last thing I said to them before they showed
up in the owner's office, furious, declaring that they could
not possibly stay in this awful place. *I* was the stated
reason. I had offended them somehow. In my defense I
started to say, "What? The very last thing I said to these
people was, if your baby needs…" but I was cut short.
Nothing like facts or truth would be allowed into this
hearing. Guilty from the moment I was hired, apparently I
would never learn.

"Monsieur, the very last thing I said to these people was…"
"It does not matter."
"But, the last thing I said to these people was…"
"It does not matter. IT DOES NOT matter. How can I get
that through to you? It does not matter!" He dismissed me
with a wave of his hand and turned to address the guests
who could not stay; the guests who had been so rudely
treated. He asked that I kindly close his office door on the
way out.

And when the guests who would not stay passed by the front desk twenty minutes later, one carrying a bottle of very good wine like a newborn, the other carrying the child like a bottle of cheap wine, they paused to glare at me—the one who had, through his rudeness, single-handedly destroyed their *honeymoon* aspirations.

I could imagine them telling their friends at home about this ghastly experience: "And then he said, 'IF there is *anything* you might need for the child, only let us know.'"
"Oh, my God," gasp their friends in unified disbelief, "that's unbelievable!"
"Yes. We spoke with the owner about that man and he apologized and gave us a bottle of good wine."
"Well, it is certainly not the kind of wound that an apology and a bottle of good wine could ever heal. I hope that, if you haven't already posted 17,000 words about this on some idiotic website, you do so soon."

I've thought about that incidence since of course, and now I realize that there really is nothing more offensive than offering to do whatever you can to assure young parents that their child's needs are a priority. My god, what was I thinking? How could I expect anyone to stay in this hotel after hearing a statement like that?

So, these are my crimes. I take restaurant reservations and say, "OK, we'll see you then!" I make beds up when asked to. And if you have a babe in arms I suggest that, if your child might have needs of any sort, you can count on us.

Looking at that list myself I can only hang my head in shame, but not so low as to prevent the noose from being placed properly upon my neck.

THE FRENCH THING

Anyone who has been working in this hotel for any length of time can tell by the look on a woman's face when she just plain does not get *the French thing*. When our dear guest arrives, she screws up her face. She walks into the office, she screws up her face; she steps into the elevator, she screws up her face; she peers into the room before entering, she enters the room cautiously, she inspects the bathroom as if we might be hiding something hideous in there, she sniffs and says, "I suppose this will have to do."

Unfortunately, despite what the owner thinks, if a guest can not appreciate the imperfect charm that is this small, privately owned French hotel, it is not our job to coax them into a new, more joyous and loftier way of thinking. When I find myself facing one of these ne'er-contents it almost never occurs to me to burst into a rousing chorus of Sunny Side of the Street in an effort to rouse them into a brighter view. And, undoubtedly if I did, that would be wrong too.

This small, privately owned hotel is not a luxury hotel. Our returning guests know that. They know they'll be carrying their own luggage and parking their own car. Many of our guests come here because of that; I've been told as much. But, guests who want luxury hotel service, without paying luxury hotel rates, may find themselves disappointed.

One evening a gentleman and his wife arrived and I knew what was going to happen from the moment he stood before the desk and refused to sit down. I mean, I knew it as soon as he asked about valet parking.

I knew it for sure when he asked for a bellman. I knew it without a doubt when he refused to touch his own luggage, merely popping the trunk open and stepping regally aside. But I knew it as sure as I know my own name when his wife stepped out of the car, wrapped herself protectively in her shawl and glared at our little hotel as if it might be contagious. Yes, you are right to be careful, Madame, I wouldn't want to catch what you have either.

There was no doubt about where this was headed when he asked to "look at" the room. At that point I would have bet that upon seeing the room she would want to check out immediately. As they followed me down the hallway in silence, I knew. After peeking in without actually stepping over the threshold, her eyes bugged out, her face scrunched up as if she smelled a foul odor. Yes, I can smell it too, Madame, and it wasn't here prior to your arrival.

The gentleman turned to me and said, "Is this the best room you've got?"
I said, "This is a very nice room."
He straightened up a bit further, if that were possible, and said, "We usually stay in luxury hotels."
I said, "Well, then you usually pay three or four times what you'll pay here."
He said, a bit huffily I thought, "What do you mean?"
I said, "I mean that, being a well-traveled and an informed individual, the price alone should have told you that this is not a luxury hotel." And, I had a very strong urge to add, 'And we don't pretend to be.' He looked at me in that way aristocrats reserve for anyone who has the audacity to be honest in their presence. His wife had not looked at me yet.

I said, "On the other hand, you really wouldn't want to stay in most of the other places that charge our modest rates."

'What do you mean by that?" he demanded.

"I'll tell you what I'll do," I said, looking him in the eye—which he didn't seem to appreciate at all—"although we have a 48 hour cancellation policy, I'll waive that for you, so you can find some other nice place to stay; some place which you might find more suitable."

"What do you mean?"

The intellectual density of people who seem to be doing quite well in this world always amazes me. I honestly believed that I'd been speaking perfectly clearly throughout this conversation. But, I was confused as to why anyone who is used to driving a Lamborghini would test drive a Peugeot and then criticize the way it looks and handles? If Lamborghini is what you want, buy the Lamborghini and stay out of what you consider to be lesser vehicles. That was my thinking. So, I said, "There are plenty of luxury hotels in San Francisco. I'll be glad to tell you how to get to any one of them which you might choose."

He studied me. "That won't be necessary," he said.

These people stayed for three nights despite the undeniable fact that they were far too good for the place. And—from the moment they arrived, until they moment they departed —they maintained a clear aristocratic superiority. They didn't belong here and they didn't like the people who did. They avoided the staff as if we might at any moment corner them in the hallway, throw an overly-friendly arm around their shoulders, pull them in closely, offer them a breathy swig from a pint of cheap whiskey and, while leering suggestively at the wife, try to convince them that we should all go skinny-dipping together sometime.

Why they stayed so long in such a miserable place I can not guess. On top of that, they were non-tippers.

When I single-handedly lugged their 32 pieces of matched Italian luggage to their room, they did not tip. When I stood in my shirt-sleeves for 15 minutes in a cold and driving rain in order to flag them a cab on a Saturday night, they did not tip. They did not tip when someone (me) brought them extra glasses. After calling down to ask that someone (me) bring them ice, they did not tip. After that was done and they called down to ask that someone (me) bring them extra towels, they did not tip.

But, there are worse guests.

WHEN I SAY 5:30 I MEAN 5:30

For some reason which I will never understand there are women in this world who take an immediate disliking to me. Perhaps I'm wrong about that; perhaps they just have an immediate disliking for everyone and everything they come into contact with; that seems like a more reasonable possibility. Nonetheless, I take the brunt of their discontent while they stand there fuming in front of me. My father recently made an observation that these days our society seems to be infested with a wide variety of groups looking for any opportunity to be offended. These women are the pace car in that race toward societal idiocy.

So, one of these lovely creatures appears like a dark and stormy vision before me while I'm on the phone. And from her demeanor I can see that she expects me to hang up the phone immediately and turn my full attention upon her—which I do not do. Instead, I handle the caller with the respect and decency any customer might expect—and I do not rush the caller, and I do not push the caller, and I do not give the caller the bum's rush. I handle the call in the same manner that I would handle any call, while she smolders in the most theatrical ways imaginable. Given that incentive, I think I deserve some credit for not purposefully dragging out the phone conversation for as long as possible.

When I am done with the phone call, I turn my eyes to the bristling storm, and she says, "Do you have any rooms that are recently renovated?"
I say, "Well, it's kind of an ongoing task. In a way, all of the rooms are continually under renovation."

She says, "But, do you have any that are RECENTLY and *fully* renovated?"

I say, "Well, not in the way you're talking about. We are continually working on the rooms to improve them."

"Because," she says, "we're staying in room 501 and it's very dark and dismal and really just shabby."

Room #501 is a very nice room and is, in fact, one of my personal favorites. I like the way it looks. But, I've been in this business for a while and I know that this woman doesn't really *get* the French thing. She doesn't understand the small, privately owned hotel thing. She likes a large room that's heartless, empty, cold, and rings loudly with the absence of any human touch—you know, something *recently and fully renovated.* And I know that there is NOTHING I can do to satisfy this woman or to turn her on to a more open minded way of looking at things.

I say, "Shabby?"

She says, "Well, you know, old furniture, old style bedspreads made of some artificial fabric… Are all your rooms like that? Don't you have *better* rooms, in case I decide I want to stay here again?"

I say, "Well, though each of the rooms is different, they are pretty much the same. I mean the owner puts the rooms together using his own aesthetic and…"

She cuts me off, "They're all the same then? Is that what you're telling me? You don't have anything better than that one we're staying in?"

"Better, no. All the rooms are different though. It's subjective; maybe there's a room which you might prefer the looks of…"

230

She cuts me off again. "All your rooms are the same?"
"In the sense that you mean, yes."

She's bug-eyed and gulping. She can hardly believe that I am telling her the truth. She looks at me for a bit with utter disapproval. Talking to me is like talking to an idiot. Any decent desk clerk would shut down the office immediately and go find a room and start renovating. But not me. I stubbornly insist that our rooms are what they are, and my comfort with that can not, by her, be understood. She changes subjects. Having failed completely at providing her with a freshly renovated room, she seeks something other way for me to satisfy her royal desires.

"Well, we have reservations in the restaurant this evening at 5:30, and I'd like to go down right now; do you think you can manage to arrange *that*?"
"Well," I look at the clock. It is ten to five. "it's going to be a busy evening down there tonight and they are probably occupied getting things ready right now. It would be better, you'd get better service and the attention you deserve, if you went down when they open, at 5:30."
"We can't go down now?"
"Things're pretty much set up to open at 5:30," I say.

So, then this… woman… goes into the lobby where her friends await the news. Because there is no wall between the office and the lobby, only a grille, I can see and hear everything she says. Her expectant friends all look up at her in a very human sort of way as she arrives. And she says this: "Well, they have no better rooms. None of them are ever renovated. They're all dull and dismal."

"What? He told you that?"

"He told me all the rooms are crap."

"Wow, he told you all the rooms are 'crap'?"

"Yeah, apparently all the rooms are crap and he couldn't care less whether we like it or not."

"Wow."

"And," she says, "AND, we can not go down to the restaurant one minute before 5:30."

"Really? Why?"

"HE says, 'When we say 5:30 we mean 5:30. They don't mean 5:10, they don't mean 5:17, THEY mean 5:30."

"Wow, he told you that?"

"When they say 5:30, they mean 5:30!" she says and throws herself into an armchair. This is a nicely attired thirty-seven year-old woman, acting like a ten year-old.

When they pass by the office on their way to the restaurant some of them don't dare to look at me, others can't resist looking to see what this monster must look like. As she passes, she glares at me the whole while.

Given the chance to hear her story, the owner of this establishment would have taken her side, of course. Why did I not comfort her? Why did I not go out of my way, even the least little bit, to shield her from the cruel fact that every single thing that occurs here on earth is not designed solely to please her? Why didn't I assure her that all she needs to do is point out her discontent and the entire world, every man, woman, and child among us will snap to and, working together in concerted effort, strain to make things more to her liking?

That's what I should have done.

And I knew it too.

But I didn't.

So, for this, of course, I should be hung.

THE PRESPONSE

I know I could probably make life easier for myself if I would only accept my dear wife's excellent advice once in a while.

It is Sunday; the one day of the week when the restaurant at the hotel is closed for dinner. It says so on our menu. I am at the desk when a woman comes in after studying the menu which is posted outside.

"Is your restaurant open for dinner this evening?" she asks.
"No, I'm sorry," I say, "Sunday is the one day they are closed for dinner."
"Oh," she says, "So, you're only open Tuesday through Friday?"
"Monday through Saturday," I say with the best smile I can come up with.
"Oh, but you're not open tonight?"
"We are closed on Sundays. Sunday is the one day they are closed for dinner."
"I was looking at the menu outside… is that the same menu you'll be serving tomorrow?" she asks.
"Soup, salad, dessert and fresh fish all change daily; the rest is standard fare," I say.
"So, that IS the menu I can expect tomorrow?"
"Basically, Madame. However, soup, salad, dessert and fresh fish all change daily… the rest, yes, is standard fare." I say with teeth firmly clenched. This is the sort of thing my dear wife tells me I can avoid by simply bending a little. And, though I know she's right, for some reason, while in the moment, I rarely bend even slightly.

"Well, I really look forward to that mushroom soup," says the woman, with a little shiver of idiotic anticipation.
"*Soup*, salad, dessert and fresh fish *all change daily*; the rest is standard fare." I say.
"Then you won't be having the mushroom soup tomorrow?" she asks with great sadness.
"It is possible. I can not say. The chef will make that decision. But, in general, soup, salad, dessert and fresh fish all change daily; the rest is standard fare." I say.
"But the other items, I mean the lamb, the rabbit, the beef, will be on the menu?" she asks.
"Soup, salad, dessert and fresh fish all change daily; *the rest* is standard fare." I say.

She raises her eyebrows and looks at me as if formulating something to say, or working on how precisely to say it, then asks cheerfully, "Will the soufflé be on the menu? I love the sound of Grand Marnier soufflé."
At this point, I believe this woman is trying to unsettle me.
"I can only guess. Soup, salad, *dessert* and fresh fish all change daily," I say.
"Will they have the salmon, do you think?"
"That I can not guess. If it is fresh, perhaps."

You would think this kind of madness is a rarity. It is not. I assure you. And, my contribution to the idiocy, a weird mix equal parts goading and stubbornness, does not help. This is the sort of conversation that my wife thinks I could avoid entirely by speaking the language of idiots while speaking with idiots. And, though I have mastery of that language— having been exposed to it for many years while in this business—I often choose not to use it.

235

When I have said something as clearly and as concisely as any human being can possibly say that thing, what more can I do? It goes against my nature to mess with it in any way or to cast it in less succinct terms, or tack on filigree, or pretend to accept that which I do not.

Later, in the evening, my lovely wife comes by to sit and chat and allow us some time to admire each other's wit, intelligence, charm, humanity (I particularly admire her commitment to finding any of that in me). I tell her the story of this woman precisely as I have just related it to you and, as predicted, she offers her usual suggestion, "Maybe you could have replied in some other form. For example, you could have simply said 'No' when she asked if the soufflé would be on the menu tomorrow."

I can not help but love this wonderful creature, my wife. She's playing with me; she's trying to get me to take a tiny little painless step toward walking without the use of my knuckles. But, I am so bloated with righteousness on this extraordinarily important matter that I can not give in, even a little, even to my playful wife, whom I adore.
"Maybe you could be a little more flexible in the way you reply to those questions," she suggests charmingly.

"There is no more precise way to explain our menu," I say crisply, but, bending just a little. "And," I add somewhat smugly, "I was not *replying* to her questions, I was PRE-plying. My answer was designed specifically to preempt further discussion. I was, in effect, answering all of her questions in one single, perfectly wrought, PRE-sponse. This seemingly simple statement," I continue to explain, "has evolved into this flawless form after years of answering the same questions over and over and over and goddamned over again. It can not be stated more simply or more clearly," I say closing the book firmly on the case.

Because my wife loves me, she says nothing… for a moment. Then she says this: "Before your next encounter you might consider PRE-vising your PRE-sponse to include a modicum of flexibility."

I know she's right of course. I tell myself she's right. And for her I want to grow. I want to evolve. I want to eventually become that slightly ditzy chatty old bastard that everybody who comes here simply adores. So, I start up the interior dialogue that is designed to change the ever-unchanging me into something more yielding, more open, more bearable, if not more likeable. The first step is to admit to myself that I'm being childish and ridiculous. So, I do that.

I'm going through the process. I've got a little internal dialogue going. I'm offering myself good advice. I'm listening carefully to my own wisdom. But, to be honest with you, I'm not sure I'm hearing a single word that I'm saying… and the ones I do hear, don't always make a lot of sense. For some things, there is no PRE-sponse.

MERCI without MERCY

SCENE: A woman stands before me at the front desk. "Can you recommend a restaurant?" she asks.
"One of the best French restaurants in this town is right here at the hotel. Our chefs are excellent. You won't have a better meal anywhere, although you could certainly pay a lot more elsewhere," I say. Throughout this chant I am being careful to display my dimples.
"I had French food last month."
"What kind of food would you like?" I smile.
"Anything."
"Anything?" I release a quiet little knowing snort.
She rolls her eyes, "Anything," she repeats with exasperation, and looks at me as if I might not understand the word. "I just want to put something in an empty stomach."

But, from years of experience I know exactly where this is leading, and I know what *anything* means. *Anything* means that the guest will systematically reject any and all of the various cuisines I offer, until, by the grace of God, I somehow finally stumble upon the one which she holds jealously protected, secretly in her heart.

"Do you eat sushi?"
"No. Sushi? Good God, NO."
"There's a pizza place across the street."
"Pizza? No."
"What kind of food would you like? It might be easier if…" I say encouragingly.
"We'd just like something close by, but good," she snaps.

"Close by, but good. There is a Mexican place on the corner…" I suggest.

"No. Is there a good little Italian restaurant which you can recommend nearby?"

"No, I'm sorry. For Italian, for real Italian, you really have to go to North Beach."

She looks at me as if this might somehow be my fault. And I can see her point of course. When they asked me— Edward, where should we put all the good little Italian restaurants?—I should have said, 'Why don't you put most of 'em in North Beach, but I'd like to have one really good one placed within a block or so of this hotel.'
I guess I just wasn't thinking at the time.

"There's nothing I could recommend near here," I say.

"There are *no* good Italian restaurants within walking distance?" She can't believe it. She looks me in the eye and is convinced that I'm holding back. She's knows there must be several good Italian restaurants in the neighborhood, but I've decided to make things difficult for her. I've decided to mess with her. I've decided to run her all over town in search of a good Italian restaurant, while I remain here, behind the desk, snickering, taking evil delight in her plight, and stuffing my face with carbonara from the place next door.

"Not that I'd recommend," I say. "You'd really have to go to North Beach."

"Well, what *do* you recommend?" she snaps.

"Thai?"

"No. Thai… no. I've never liked Thai."
Why did I not guess that? I ask myself.

Against my own better judgment I let out a little laugh. I recognize square one when I see it again. I take a deep breath. I smile. I pause. I try to find the joy in this.

"What kind of food *would* you like?" I ask again, without sighing, and without barking.
"How's this place across the street?"
"I've never been there."
"You've never eaten in the restaurant across the street from you?"
"That's right."
"Well have you HEARD anything about it?"
"They are our neighbors, Madame," I say.

My words are overflowing with a message which no one could possibly miss but which somehow gets lost in the distance between my lips and her ear. She waits. I shrug in a manner which says, 'Madame, you are placing me in a difficult position.' She continues to stare, so I say, "It would be difficult for me to recommend any place in which I haven't eaten."
"Well, thank you. Thank you very much," she says sarcastically. "What is your name?"
"My name is Edward."
"Well, thank you very much, EDWARD, you've been utterly useless," she says.

I say nothing, recognizing that it fits in so nicely with the utterly useless theme. And I smile an utterly useless little smile.

240

As an employee at the hotel, I'm not allowed to say anything which every fiber of my being urges me to say in a situation like this. There are many things I could say, but, all of them would be inappropriate; correct and perfectly justifiable, but inappropriate. In the desk clerk-as-peon/guest-as-royalty arrangement, any response I could come up with would be considered out of line.

For my bullheaded unwillingness to give this guest what she asked for—to either recommend a place in which I have never set foot or a good Italian place within 30 paces of where we stood at that moment—I should, of course, be hung. Had the hanging taken place *before* her arrival however, it would have been a kindness to both of us.

SOMETHING-FUSION

The exact opposite of this was the young man who came into the office one evening with a precise wish. He sat down and asked my dear wife, with a straight face, if she could recommend a good restaurant that served good Mediterranean-Fusion.

Mediterranean-Fusion? Neither my good wife nor I knew exactly what Mediterranean-Fusion was, and confessed as much. After recovering from the shock of that, the young man started to explain that it was Mediterranean cuisine but with a fusion kind of aspect to it. He stopped midway into the explanation however. Apparently the blank look in our eyes made him realize the futility of his efforts. I'm fairly sure he couldn't have heard the raucous laughter that was bouncing around in my mind, thunderous and demanding as it was.

After the kid left frustrated by our total lack of hipness—I told my dear wife I'd be willing to bet that he himself didn't know what Mediterranean fusion was, and I voiced my suspicions about what it might be.
"It arrives at the table on a large white square plate; there is raspberry coulis drizzled in random patterns around the periphery, and maybe a cream colored drizzle intertwined as well; in the center, in a pool of some gooey—your choice—white sticky stuff with balsamic sore-spots or brownish yuck with capers, there is a rounded glob of who-knows-what, a mound at any rate, with three fried sea bass fins sticking out of its sides at a jaunty angle; this mound is topped with a dollop of caviar, covered by a small weird

haystack of unnamable finely shredded greenery (though, much to the delight of everyone at the table, some will be laced with either carrot or leek) and sticking out from that there is a single, deep-fried, crinkle-cut potato chip something like the main-sail of a tall ship. Near one edge, there is a whole, tiny, strangely colored, freshly imported turnip sliced and fanned open, and in one corner about half a teaspoon, no more, of jelled currant-apple sauce—by whatever name they may give it—made on the premises fresh each day by the executive chef himself, whom everybody eating there seems to know personally."
My dear, insightful wife laughed a lovely bell-like laugh and added these clever words: "Sixty-seven dollars."

This was not the first time that we've read each other's minds precisely. What a pleasure it is to be in love with your wife. Still, the kid went away frustrated, thinking we were dull and stupid and out of touch, which we are admittedly, and with great pleasure.

Obviously this is all sour grapes. The Mediterranean-Fusion places in this town are all packed every night with people sitting, crammed in like sardines, and screaming like nestlings. They couldn't be more pleased with things; the atmosphere, the food, the service, themselves. Who are we to question such a phenomenon? Throwbacks to a dull and miserable past, we still cling to the antiquated idea that restaurants should have something to do with good food, served in generous quantity, at a reasonable price, and that a bottle of respectable wine should not be seen as yet another opportunity to screw the customer.

DECEPTION

Mr. Bouchard arrives, and from the moment he sits down opposite my wife he has a continuous monologue going about how he has been deceived before by booking other hotels over the internet. And at that point, given my experience in this trade, I don't know why I don't stand up, grab the guy by the scruff of his neck and the seat of his pants and simply toss him out into the street, but I don't. So, it goes on for several minutes until my wife breaks in to assure him that we are what we say we are, a small privately owned French hotel; we have nothing to hide. He says, "That's a relief to hear, several times I've been deceived by websites declaring their place to be everything that they are not." He then says, "I look forward to dining in your restaurant this evening, that's the whole reason I've come here really, well, a good part of the reason I chose your establishment."

My very dear wife is now in the awkward position of having to tell this gentleman that the restaurant is closed on this evening, so I step in.

I say, "Unfortunately, the restaurant is closed on Sundays."

More startling news has never been conveyed. This can be read in the man's face; the bulging eyes and the raised eye brows particularly. "Well, that's just exactly the sort of thing I'm talking about!" he declares. "I looked over your website very carefully and NOWHERE on your website does it say *that*. It's the whole reason I came here! This is EXACTLY the sort of thing I'm talking about."

We say nothing, allowing the man to cool down.

Instead, he goes on. "I just looked at your menu outside and IT says nothing about being closed on Sundays."

"It does say that," I assure him.

"It most certainly does NOT. I looked at the menu very carefully, and for a very long time, and it says nothing about your restaurant being closed on Sundays."

"It does," I say.

"Well, I challenge you to show me where!" he says rising from his seat.

So, I take him outside and show him the menu.

"Well, it doesn't say so on your website, and that's how I found this place," he tells me without apology.

"I'm sure it says so on the website as well," I say holding the door open for him.

He goes storming back inside and directly into the office. As I enter the office he's saying to my wife, "Now, I've lost all confidence in you. I don't know what to believe or who I can trust any more. I really have to see the room before I sign anything."

I take him to one of the two rooms available and he starts on the same tirade with me while standing just inside the door. We have deceived him. The fact that the restaurant is closed on Sundays is 'purposefully undisclosed' on our website. He has looked over that website carefully, and NOWHERE does it say that the restaurant is closed on Sundays.

After what Christ himself would consider enough of that, I question these accusations. He's basically calling us liars, and I don't hold a fondness in my heart for anyone who does that.

He concludes his rant by saying, "Typical French; I never should have booked this place!" I show him to the elevator and put him in and before letting the door close I say this: "If I'm not mistaken your last name is French."
I go down the steps to give the man some privacy and once inside the office I immediately draw up our website. I go to the restaurant page which clearly states that the restaurant is closed on Sundays. I press print.

He arrives and does not sit down. He says, "I'd like to SEE where on your website it says your restaurant is closed on Sunday. I'd like you to show me that."
I simply hand him the page which I just printed out. And while he's looking at that, never one to overplay my hand, I swivel the computer screen toward him so he can have a look at the thing itself. It hardly matters; he's decided he doesn't want to stay. He wants his pre-authorization cancelled. This is EXACTLY the kind of thing he was telling us about. He demands that we destroy his file. He's sorry he ever heard of this place. He'll never set foot in this place again.
My wife, in her gentle and kindly manner tries to convince him to stay. She offers to show him another room. No, he just wants to get out of here. So we cancel his reservation and he leaves in a huff.

Because the town is thoroughly packed and every hotel completely booked, he is back in about twenty minutes. I see him coming through the door and step out to greet him in the hallway.
"We weren't good enough for you five minutes ago, we're probably not good enough for you now," I say.

My dear wife—knowing that the owner will hold us responsible if we don't rent a room to a man who five minutes earlier refused to stay, calling us liars to our faces, while declaring the place unsuitable—encourages the gentleman to have a seat. Yes, that's the way we do business. After you insult us, demand a refund, call this establishment a den of thieves and go stomping out the front door muttering that you'll never set foot in this miserable place again, we welcome you back with open arms. We hope this time we might come closer to fulfilling your expectations.

The gentleman goes to his room, and some time later he comes back down and he apologizes to me. Naturally, or naturally for me anyway, I am tempted to say something. I'd like to offer the man what I believe is good advice. For example I'd like to say, "You know, if one doesn't conduct oneself like an unbearable ass to begin with, one rarely has to apologize for one's behavior." But I don't do that, though I think it would be instructive. I don't do it because I know that the owner will find some way to twist that around and use it against me.

Despite his 48 years in this business, the owner somehow remains unable to see that there are good guests and there are bad guests, and that there are morons in this world, and that this particular moron is also some kind of a revolving idiot, and we don't need that around here infecting the rest of our guests. Nor would the owner see that we—my wife, who is always courteous and nice, and me (about whom I can say nothing good)—did the best we could with that man.

And, in the inevitable trial when choosing to side with his dedicated employees or some guy who walked out of this establishment in a huff while calling us all a bunch of liars, the owner would side with the 'guest'. So, the man is persuaded to stay and I know without a doubt precisely where this is headed. Hand me that rope.

A similar thing happened recently where the guests did not like the room they are slated to stay in. We're packed stem to stern, but I go down and manipulate the files of incoming guests for five or ten minutes so that they might have another room. I take them to that room and they don't like it either. I have shown them the only two rooms I can offer. Short of starting construction immediately up on the roof, I don't know what my other options might be. They don't like either of the rooms; we're packed, the town is packed. So, I say, very kindly, "Although we have a 48 hour cancellation policy, I'll let that slide if you would like to try to find somewhere else to stay." This they find offensive. But they keep it a secret to themselves. They stay for two nights with this secret hidden somewhere deep within. They stay in one of the rooms *they don't like* with this resentment simmering inside for the length of their stay.

More than a month later—this is how long my offensive behavior has gnawed on them—they complain. The offense was not that I made Herculean efforts to move things around in order to offer them another room to consider, it's that I offered to let them escape the contractual arrangement by which we could extract the full price of that room whether they stayed or not.

That I should suggest to them that they might find a room more to their liking elsewhere was the offense.

"We'll take a room we don't like, but it'll be your fault!"

Of course it will.

IN THE BRAZILIAN MANNER

A French couple arrives packed in the Brazilian manner1, with nine bags, each of which is larger and heavier than a standard fully loaded American refrigerator, and none of which they themselves would ever even consider touching. I invite them into the office and ask them if they would like to sit down. They do not wish to sit down. Apparently my addressing them in English has put them out of a sitting down mood. So, while they stand there, looking down upon me disapprovingly from far far above, I check them in. I load their luggage onto a cart, escort them to the elevator, and show them to their room.

In the room, I off-load their baggage. The gentleman—15 years younger than me, no doubt better educated, more well-traveled, and great deal more successful than I will ever be—offers no assistance. He stands there and watches as I off-load their luggage. As I am doing that they ask for a wake-up call at 5 A.M, in French.
"Five A.M," I reply in English, before heading back downstairs to the office.

Repeating it in my native tongue is my way of marking the thing in my mind so that I don't forget it. I am not trying to insult them further by using English yet again in their esteemed presence.

---

1 The lithe young ladies of Brazil seem to have a fear of leaving anything at home when they travel and, judging from the weight of them, their perfectly matched, overly-large, luggage seems to be crammed full of bricks.

But, had I slapped them both across the face, the offense could not have been greater.

When I arrive back at the desk there is a message waiting, and one line is ringing. I pick up the line, and it is these very same French guests; they have decided that they can not stay in the room which was assigned to them; they want another room. They want something in the front of the building; they'd like to see the street. I check the chart, and there is, by miracle, one room which might accommodate them without moving imminent arrivals around too much. It is located one floor below them, in the front. I tell them I will be right up. First I must set the wake-up call for 5 A.M. in the new room, and I must change the file, the chart, the room list and the maid's list to reflect their move. Before I go though I check the message left on our voice mail. The message is these same people requesting, in French, that they be placed in another room. They explain, in French, that they do not like to be in the back of the building.

I grab a luggage cart and go up to their room, where they are standing by impatiently. Their bags are sitting in the place where I unloaded them ten minutes earlier. The couple does not appear to be ten minutes happier.

They watch somewhat disgruntled, it would appear, as I load their bags—which seem to have multiplied both in number and weight during that brief rest—onto the cart. After asking them for the keys to the room they are standing in—a request which apparently offends them—I take them to the elevator where, enshrouded in a chilly funereal silence, we go down to the new room.

They follow me down the hall as if in mourning. I open the door to that room and let them step in and sniff the place a bit... which they do. After they poke around as if we might be hiding something awful, or maybe just shameful, they give me the nod, and I push the luggage cart in and unload their bags while they look regally on. I hand them the keys to the new room. They remind me, in French, of their wake-up call. I smile and run downstairs to the office, where the phone is ringing as I unlock the door.

It is them again.

They have decided, they tell me in French, that they want to see yet another room. I look at the chart. I tell them, in English—the language of savages—that this will take some doing and I will call them back once it has been arranged. Apparently, I don't understand just how offensive, short-sighted and selfish it is for this small, privately owned French hotel not to have an endless supply of vacant rooms available from which they might choose. Their silence informs me of this however, before they hang up.

This move requires moving several guests who have not yet arrived and extends on into moving guests who will not be arriving for days. It sounds like a simple matter but it requires care, changing files, changing the chart, changing the room list, changing the maids' list, erasing the wake-up call for the room they *were* in and setting it for the room they *will be* (hopefully and finally) going into. I make NONE of those adjustments however. By this point I know enough about these guests. I grab the key to the new room, grab the luggage cart and head up stairs in the elevator.

It's the same as before. There they are waiting, this time in a kind of barely restrained aristocratic fury. A cold assessment is made of me as I enter into their presence, and I'm found lacking. It's just disgusting the way I drag my feet.

I say to them this: "Let me take you to this room and show it to you first. IF you like it, then I will come back and get your bags." And that is what I do. It's another funeral procession to the next room. They look at the room, they shrug, they reluctantly give me the go-ahead to bring their baggage; they've surrendered. Apparently, this is the best we can do. When I return with their luggage, they watch as I unload each bag, none of which have gotten any lighter. I ask them for the keys to the other room and then skittle downstairs and begin the necessary alteration of files.

While I am in the midst of this, the phone rings.

They have decided that they really much prefer the first room they were in. When I show up at their door with the luggage rack, my attitude is less effusive than they would expect. I don't flutter; I don't mince; I don't bow deeply enough or thank them profusely enough for the great honor it has been to haul them and their goddamned baggage all over the goddamned hotel and, now, back again. In turn, they neither smile nor offer me thanks, in any form or language, for my cooperation in the madness. They make no apology for being of a superior race, of course, and my lack of apology to them, for being a savage, stings. If indeed I have been assigned to be their personal servant for the duration of their stay, as they have, until this moment, assumed, they really must insist upon someone else. They want someone who might genuinely appreciate the great privilege they offer; someone who would show a little more gratitude; someone who'll whistle while he works; someone who has nothing else to do in life but move them around endlessly from room to room until the end of time, and finds his joy in that.

Ah well, as they say. My poor attitude is reported, next day, to the owner... which comes as a complete surprise to me. I am called into his office to face these gentle people who, sitting comfortably in chairs imported from their native land and speaking comfortably in their native tongue, point at me—as if to confirm that I am indeed the one—and, since I could not possibly understand a word of French, a brief conversation concerning me takes place, in French, while I stand there. From the tone alone I deduce that they were not pleased with my performance.

The owner does not get the complete story, but what he gets is all that he needs in order to rule on the matter. Why I have selected these wonderful visitors to treat so cruelly he can not understand. My attitude toward these guests is inappropriate and unacceptable and who knows what all else... words can't be found. And, to begin the list that never ends would be futile. All that he can see is my shamefully flawed anti-social, perhaps psychotic, nature.

Meanwhile, they blink like sheep, in pure innocence, while I stand there irredeemable; smelling of sulfur, so tightly held in Satan's grip that I make no attempt to conceal the fact.

The owner and God both know that I refuse to change. and will never express contrition. Willingness to change has been driven entirely out of my being by a proud, ever-darkening indifference. I wait until I am leaving that office before I either roll my eyes or begin to cuss. Behind my back, the owner's soft consoling cooing nags me even as I flee. Like holy water, it burns my soul.

Nevertheless, I'm still here. As far as anyone can figure—and we've all given the matter nearly endless thought—I ain't goin' nowhere. Desk clerks are like drummers; a good desk clerk is hard to find, a bad desk clerk is hard to get rid of, and I'm the Rasputin of this small, privately owned French hotel. Nothin' you do will kill me; though drenched in my own blood, I just keep crawlin' back.

More accurately, maybe I should say, At least I can't be fired for offering to supply young parents with anything their baby might require during their stay (no matter how brief). I can't be fired for hauling a French couple and every possession they have here on earth from one room to another and then to a third and back to the original room in sullen silence. And, apparently, I can't even be fired for marrying the owner's daughter and making her happy, although, certainly if such an act could be found criminal, this is the city for it. There are times when I feel that I could be replaced however. I could be replaced, for example, with an egotistical, self-serving, twenty-seven year old sponge. I know that, because I have been.

I once lived with a woman whose greatest blessing was her twenty-seven year old precious son. Our arrangement was that I paid rent; I mowed the lawn, I fixed the washing machine when it needed it; I took out the garbage; I bought food, I prepared meals, and I did the dishes. When she was in trouble, I responded and helped her out of trouble. Her son—her twenty-seven year old dearest darling son—paid no rent; he mowed no lawn, he fixed no washing machines; he took out no garbage, he bought no food, prepared no meals and did no dishes. And, when she was in trouble and called for help, he handed the phone to me.

One day, just in casual conversation, I remarked, "You know, I think there are too many people living here." The woman looked at me. She did not blink, she did not ponder; she simply said, "You're right. You have to go."

She just tossed me out like the rent-paying, lawn-mowing, washing machine-fixing, garbage-hauling, food-buying, dinner-preparing, dishes-doing, ever-caring rat that I was. Draw what conclusions you will from that; at this small, privately owned French hotel, I find myself once again in that same position.

And, sometime soon, I expect the very same results.

THE OTHER SIDE OF THAT BRAZILIAN COIN

There was a Russian man staying here and he appeared at the office door sometime late in the evening. He was furious. The radiator in his room was making a lot of noise and he couldn't sleep. He was tired. He had come a long way. He wanted to sleep. That was all he wanted, was to sleep. He was VERY tired. But he could not sleep. The sounds coming from that radiator were keeping him awake. "I understand," I assured him. "I'll be up in a minute."

So, I went down and got some rags and I went up to his room and I did what I normally do; I turned off the valve and I bled the radiator, and I cleaned out the relief valve. When I turned it back on, it still made a lot of noise, so I apologized and I told him, "I'll go downstairs and see if there is any possibility of moving you to another room. But, you know, it's fairly unlikely, the place is packed solid right now and you're staying for a long time. I don't know what the odds are, but I'll see what I can do."
He said, "I just want to get some sleep. It is not an unreasonable thing to ask."
I could not have agreed more.

So, I went down to the office and I looked very carefully at the chart—and I have to say that I'm pretty good at this—but I could not find any way that I could move that poor man from that room. I tried. It just wasn't there, or, if it was, I couldn't see it. But, I continued trying. I thought, maybe there is something here and I'm just not seeing it. So, I was looking very carefully at the chart for the twenty-seventh time when he appeared in the doorway and sat down heavily across from me. "One second," I said, and went back to staring at the unmoving chart.

"Any luck?" he asked.
"Phhhhhh!" I said, and threw up my hands.
"What do you mean, Phhhhhh?" he asked.
I looked at him with the full weight of my job pressing down upon my soul, and I said, "I mean this: Every day of my life I have these things; things that I would LIKE TO fix, and WANT TO fix, so that people like you are pleased, but I'm helpless. There's simply nothing I can do for you. I'd really like to help you, honestly I would, but I can't. There's just nothing I can do. THAT'S what I mean by Phhhhh!"
He nodded. He knew exactly what I meant.

And that good man stood up, and he shook my hand, and he said, "Thank you for trying." And, from that moment on, that Russian gentleman treated me like a friend.

Contrast him with the man who appeared before me one morning complaining bitterly that the heater kept him and his wife up all night with the noise. I apologized and said, "I'll go up right now and drain the thing." And he said this: "For all the good that'll do *us!*"

But, there is almost nothing I (or anyone else for that matter) can do about a clanging radiator *after the fact*, and the implication that I was personally involved somehow—perhaps hidden somewhere in their room and sneaking out occasionally to bang on the thing for my own selfish entertainment—is wrong.

NOT THE PLUMBER

The people in #308 are discontent. He has come down to the office to tell me that their room is cold; the heater doesn't heat their room. I say, "I'll come up and look at it." He says, "You mean you are coming into our room?" There is nothing I can say to this. I get up and follow him out of the office.
"Where are you going?" he asks accusatorily.
"I'm going to look at your heater…"
"Do you need to come into our room?"
There is nothing I can say to this. Or rather, the only things I can think of to say in response would be judged by any civilized person as unacceptable. But, I am at a loss when I find myself having to explain to a grown man that in order to look at an object, to evaluate the problem with it and to fix it, I must be in the same room with it.

So, I go to his room and I discover that the heater is off. I tell him, "The heater is off." I turn it on. I do not tell him that in order for a heater to work, it must be on. That would be overstepping the line. I remove the relief valve and I say, "I'll need to go into your bathroom to rinse this." He follows me into the bathroom and watches me carefully as I rinse the relief valve. Otherwise, who knows what I might really be doing in there.

Later—this is the kind of night it is, this is the kind of guest he is—he calls down to say that there is no hot water in the shower. I say, "I'm sure there is." I reflect briefly upon the many thousands of times guests have declared that they have nearly lost a layer of skin because our water is too hot.

I say, "Let it run for a bit; I'm sure you'll get hot water."
He says, "I am telling you, there is no hot water. I can not take a shower."
I say, "Would you like me to come up and look at it?"
He says, "There is no hot water. I am telling you. I can not take a shower."
I say, "I'll be up in a minute."

I go up to #308 and I knock. He lets me in and says, "There is no hot water in the tub and I can not take a shower."
I start to head into the bathroom and he says, "Where are you going?" I can not think of any suitable answer to this question. There is an open door; it leads into the bathroom, I'm heading in that direction. My guess, pure speculation of course, is that the tub is in that bathroom.

I go into the bathroom and run water in the sink. It is hot. I go to the tub and run water in the tub, it is warm. I stand there for about four minutes while the water gets steadily hotter. Meanwhile, he is leaning in the doorway and keeping a close eye on me. When my hand turns red I say, "There's hot water."
Without moving from his position he says, "It is not hot."
I say, "It is hot." I show him my red hand. "It's hot."
"THAT," he declares, still without having felt the water himself, "is not hot. How can I take a shower in that?"
"Well, it's as hot as I can get it," I say and start to leave their room.
He steps in front of me, "Where are you going? How can I take a shower with no hot water?"
"The water is as hot as I can make it," I say and step around him.

What he fails to understand is that I am neither a plumber nor a magician. He does seem to detect the subtler message however, that I have no regrets.

"Where are you going?" he demands. "I cannot take a shower. This water is not hot. Where are you going?" There is nothing I can say or do in this instance, or if there is, I can't think of it. I say the water is hot and he says it's not: stalemate. I'm not sure how, or even if, the matter can be successfully resolved. I know one thing for sure though: I'll be found guilty for this event.

And I know this as well:
I sincerely hope the stupid bastard scalded himself.

Of the several types of somewhat-less-than-perfect guests, this gentleman fit all categories. Beyond demanding, he was a dabbler in petty crime, hoping to accumulate enough verifiable discontent to warrant a free stay. He was also woefully misinformed about the likelihood of that—if I happened to be at the helm when he checked out.

From his actions, he was also insane, though not nearly as insane as some.

MR. BLEMISH

As a general rule, if the person calling to make a reservation sounds clearly insane we have no rooms available, but it's easy to be fooled over the phone, and the others all rent rooms to the wildly insane more often than I do. But, I have the advantage of having picked up more than my share of extreme wackos in bars before, and readily recognize the commonest traits. My discernment is so fine that I can actually detect the difference between a highly-strung, perpetually frustrated businesswoman stretched to her limit and a psychotic whose spiritual emanations are fluctuating maybe just a bit too erratically between orange and green. But, it's easy to be fooled.

It's especially easy to be fooled by scrutinizing someone standing at the front door, over the security monitors. I've buzzed in many people who looked fine in the monitor but by the time they've walked sixteen steps from the front door to the front desk they've transformed into something most regrettable. And so it was with Mr. Blemish. Worse yet, though we had no way of telling at the time, he was one of those people who strongly believed that if he paid for a short period of time in advance, at check-in, he could then stay as long as he liked without any further expenditure. Once he was firmly ensconced, our challenge was to re-educate him on the matter of payment; but there was nothing we could do about his sanity.

In the beginning we called him Mr. Blemish, then just Blemish, then that guy in #304, and, ultimately, either that rat, which was my dear wife's take, the bastard in #304, which was mine, or, as the others had it, simply 304. When it got to that stage, the words, Three Oh Four, actually produced a bad taste in my mouth whenever I was forced to utter them; and hearing them spoken by others made me cringe.

However, at first Mr. Blemish seemed OK. He was clever. He had a nimble mind. So many guests arrive here seemingly with no other task in life than to trudge slowly ever-onward, dragging along behind themselves huge dark heavy bags on squeaky wheels, that most of us found Blemish refreshing. A little spark, a little surprise, a little peculiarity is always welcome. I'm not saying I liked Blemish going in—I don't like anybody going in—but he was more entertaining than most.

Blemish was fairly widely knowledgeable, and by that I mean that I supposed when he quoted a long poetic passage to me in the ancient Nordic tongue, he wasn't just making it up as he went along, and his free-wheeling political views were acceptable—unfettered post-nationalistic, free-market anarchism. Blemish didn't seem to think he was the only clear thinker on the planet either, and I've always liked that in the sane as well as the insane. Mr. Blemish was, as far as I could tell, an OK kind of guest, despite his membership in the Fortean Society. Though he insisted that we are fished for from above—his belief that the pyramids were cast is a dearly held, somewhat wacky concept of my own. And then there's that NEVER ODD OR EVEN thing.

He was certainly unique, and, he didn't need four nose rings to pull it off.

On occasion he would stop in and talk, and laugh at his own undeniable brilliance or mumbled little witticism to himself in response to something he had himself just said or thought he had just said or might yet say. What is a little frightening is how often I got it. I was right out there with him. I liked Blemish for a very long time. In fact, I liked him until the very day he stopped paying for his room.

Until that moment I enjoyed the casual, assured delivery of his somewhat oblique observations... a delivery which should have been telling—given my experience—but was somehow overlooked. Oblique observations are, of course, the natural tool of so-called comedians, genuine geniuses, fully-committed alcoholics and the purely, the proudly, the loudly, the frenetically insane. And, as time went on, either a transformation took place or the scales had fallen from our eyes, either way the full glorious Mr. Blemish emerged.

At that point it became clear that Mr. Blemish had gone just a bit beyond clever, had maybe overshot clever by a mile or two. My concern was that maybe he wasn't clever at all, but merely stark raving mad. If Mr. Blemish was adrift out there somewhere beyond the rational sphere, there was very little we could do about it. Unfortunately, that awakening came long after signatures were in place all around and the guy had keys to the place and had been fully entrenched in his room for a while. Our hope then, was that he would maintain the illusion of sanity in the presence of our other guests, and make occasional periodic contact with reality long enough to pay his bill without too much nagging. What I didn't know was that others on staff had begun to dislike Blemish almost from the beginning.

At breakfast he wanted not four, but only three, pieces of toast, and they could not be stacked up in the usual manner, but had to be arranged in a star-like pattern. "Upon this I am compelled to insist," he was quoted as having said. He would pout like Harpo Marx until the plate arrangement met his satisfaction. So, the servers at breakfast did not like serving Mr. Blemish.

The maids enjoyed cleaning his room even less.

Let me make it clear right here that some very fine people are slobs when it comes to the way they treat a hotel room. Some seem to think that such behavior is required of them. When I worked in Del Mar, movie stars of various levels came and went, and when they went the room was knee deep in shredded clothing, paper bags, apple cores, carry-out containers, garbage, and a single cast-off pink satin high heel shoe. When they came again, we were delighted to see them, but that was tinged somewhat by what we knew of their slovenly habits. I would name names but *Five Easy Pieces* is still a pretty good little film and I still find what's-her-name interesting to look at despite the fact that she now touts yoghurt, the primary selling point of which seems to be its ability to unclog drains.

Eventually, having alienated everyone on staff by one means or another, Mr. Blemish determined that it was time to declare, in a somewhat lengthy, convoluted, partly rational, hand-written epistle (the preferred method of the truly insane), that he liked the place so much, and felt "such a part of the family here", that he "might just stay on, well, why not (?) forever".

Those were his exact words.

Maybe we were reading between the lines but everybody here thought the word *forever* sounded like a threat.

It was at about this point—the declaration of his undying love for the hotel—that he decided, no doubt as a token of that great love, to stop paying for his room.

According to the State of California, refusal to pay one's hotel bill is not reasonable cause to eject a guest once he has established a foothold. And, should you choose to attempt it, the full weight and power of the State may come down upon you. In their eyes, a guest who refuses to pay needs to be protected from the hotelier's greed. According to the State such a guest really hasn't done much more than overstay his welcome... and that is no crime... although, admittedly, in some circles, it might be considered a nuisance. This is as I understand it.

Legalities aside, the non-paying insane can be a clingy sort of folk, and it's a difficult task to remove one from his lair without a lot of ranting and raving and screaming and the throwing about of heavy, moveable, solid plaster objects, and the loud sputtering of unwarranted, sometimes foul, often vulgar, typically grandiose, and completely false accusations. If there is one thing upon which the owner and I can agree, it is that our sane paying guests don't really need to witness that sort of thing.

When Mr. Blemish showed up in front of the desk one evening talking about gold coins which he had hidden in his room and which had, by his account, disappeared, I winced. When he insinuated that one of our maids had taken those coins, I stopped wincing and stood up and made Mr. Blemish do a little wincing of his own.

"Wait!" I commanded, "You're saying one of our maids took these coins?"

"I beseech you to consider these shameful facts: I had seventeen gold ducats in un-circulated condition in a drawer of the desk that resides unassumingly below the somewhat cluttered window that looks grimly down upon what you would not presume to label a garden but in which, nevertheless, green things are known to struggle for a meager, futureless existence. I'm not saying prosper…I…"

I stopped him in mid-sentence. "And?"

"And…I tell you sir, that this in and of itself is undeniable. You dare not question me on this sensitive matter. How do I put this in a loving way? Confess at least this, that your maid, and I believe you know the one of whom I speak— old with jet-black pageboy-cropped coif—has, perhaps inadvertently, but most assuredly, mind you, absconded with these seventeen, extremely valuable, gold ducats."

"She's been working here for over twenty years, Mr. Blemish. She has never taken anything from any room and she has never been *accused* of taking anything from any room." In fact, the poor old woman had a habit of leaving things behind; dust rags most frequently.

"Well, sir, *now* she has. And I must insist that these fine and rare coins be returned. Is it really necessary to add, forthwith? And be mindful of how this me you answer."

"Let's go look at your room," I said coming around to his side of the desk.

"What? Why that seems to me entirely unnecessary."

"Forthwith," I said. "Let's go."

In his room Mr. Blemish started throwing clothes and books and things around in an overly dramatic search for the missing coins. I stood by and watched as he mumbled to himself and scattered things about wildly.

"Could they be here? No. Under here perhaps? No. How about under here? Nooooo! Where could they be? Where could they be?"

Once in a while he would stop, pull himself upright, turn his face toward me and glare, but to no effect. Then, opening an old beaten leather satchel, which sat on top of the cluttered desk, he came across the coins. There were three of them; they were not gold (as far as I could tell) and they were far from un-circulated (as far as I could tell); and since I had no idea what a ducat was, I could not judge that, but knowing him as I then did, they weren't that either.

"Those are the coins?" I asked.

"Yes, I don't know how they might have found their way into this unexpected ambuscade. Perhaps this dear maid removed them in an effort to secure them in a way she deemed to be more abstentious," he said.

"You said there were 17 gold coins…" I said coldly.

"Yes, I was down in Bimini not too very long ago—lovely weather the whole time—and I had with me, at that time, these 17 gold—un-circulated, mind you, sir—ducats. They were rare and just exceptional examples of the period in which they were—well, I hesitate to use the word in mixed company—struck. (He winked) I then decided that I would not carry them with me in my travels—thinking better of it, the rigors being what they are—but instead…"

"These are the coins?" I demanded.

"Yes."

"Mr. Blemish," I said, "you owe this hotel something in the order of $1600. Now you are accusing *our* maids of stealing from you. That's as much as we can put up with. You must leave here. I'd like to see you leave tonight."

"Why, whatever, sir, could you possibly have—please tell me, I beseech you—in mind?"

"Our guests *pay* to stay here. You have not paid in many days. Ergo, you must go."

I left Mr. Blemish. Closing the door on his madness, I went to our little rooms to eat dinner while my wife sat in at the office. Naturally, with fork suspended between plate and lip, the phone rang and I was called to the office. When I arrived, Mr. Blemish was there with a suitcase, staring wildly at my wife.

"Oh, I'm glad that you've come," he said, "I wanted you to be here to witness this," and turning the suitcase upside down, he opened it and spilled a pile of ragged, torn, wrinkly and dirty clothes onto the floor in front of us. He stood there and glared at us with his hands on his hips.

'What do you make of that?!" he said.

Neither my wife nor I spoke.

"You've taken my soul, you might just as well take this!" he declared and disappeared.

Joan Crawford couldn't have done it better.

Since I hate idiocy, I went and got a large plastic garbage bag, bagged the damned stuff—using a stick of some sort—took it immediately back upstairs, and knocked on 304. When he opened the door I handed it to him. "You can leave right now, and I will not call the sheriff's office," I told him. "Do you understand me?"

He glared at me in the blistering affirmative.

Several hours later, when the Sheriff's officers arrived, he was still in his room.

He did quite well at first, speaking with the boys in blue — and, for a while there, I could see that they thought it might actually be my problem—but, he could not maintain the illusion. Soon he slipped into a sing-song soliloquy about wealth and the unmarked inner struggles of those deemed irresponsible in an ever-more-grasping world—during which he looked for understanding in the eyes of the sheriffs. While going on about "thieving maids and the vile underlings who spring like lions to their unwarranted defense" he locked eyes with me personally. The cops both looked at me, rolled their cold grey eyes, and listened to him with remarkable patience, until he had reached an end. I was impressed. When he had finished his plea, they told Mr. Blemish to pack up his things, he was leaving that very moment.

I interrupted to say, "You know, it's kind of late now and it might be difficult for him to find a place to stay. It's OK with me if he stays tonight."

The officers looked at me askance; not really as though I had just wasted their time, but that was certainly part of it. "Are you sure? You don't have to…" one said.

"It's kind of late, and he might find it difficult…"

They made Mr. Blemish promise that he would be out by 9 AM on the following morning. They told him, "IF this gentleman, who is kind enough to let you stay here, calls us back again tonight, we'll be taking you away in the back of our car, and you don't want that."

By 9 AM the following day Mr. Blemish was gone.

He's been kind enough to stay in touch though.

From time to time we still receive postcards from various parts of the world, with lovely little, nicely composed poetic threats carved into the backs of them. The message is always pretty much the same. One day, he promises us in flowery terms, we will pay for his humiliation.

The frightening thing about these missives is that they are always addressed to me… you know, the kind gentleman who allowed him stay an extra night.

HOW DOORS AND DOORBELLS WORK

It would be less than honest of me not to include myself in the INSANE category, and I think, if I haven't already, I can prove it here now. I'll be doing that throughout the remainder of this book as well, so that the point is made decisively. And, though I won't argue that I've been driven to my insanity by guests, any reasonable person could see how I might reasonably make that claim.

One night, the last couple from the restaurant departed leaving their credit card behind on the table. The waiter, a young French fellow, arrived fleet of foot at the office saying, "Those guests, those people…they left their credit card." Since I wanted some air anyway, I took the opportunity to get up and run out after them. I managed to get their attention near the far end of the block. Had I any brains I suppose I'd have taken the credit card with me (but I didn't) and simply handed it to them… so draw what conclusion you can from that. The good customers and I walked back toward the hotel where the waiter remained waiting, outside, under the marquee.

The credit card was returned to its owner with little ceremony, and because I lock the front door at 9 pm, the waiter and I found ourselves locked out. I was reaching into my pocket to get the keys, when he rang the doorbell. And I said this: "Have you ever read Alice's Adventures in Wonderland?"
He rang the doorbell again and said, "Yes, I think so, why?"

And I said, "It does little good for you to ring with us both on the same side of the door."
Having said that, I stepped forward and inserted my key.

"In order for that to have any real effect," I continued, "we should be on opposite sides of the door."
"Yes, yes," he said, I thought perhaps somewhat peevishly.
"For example," I continued while turning the key, "If you were on the outside, and I was on the inside, you might ring the bell and I could let you in…"

I opened the door and he pushed by me.
"OR," I continued, following him as he moved rapidly down the hallway, "if you were on the *inside* and *I* were on the outside, *I* could ring the doorbell, and *you*…"

At this point, he was so far down the hallway that I was forced to shout. "COULD LET *ME* IN."

Apparently, he found no humor in it.

I find no humor in swindlers, no matter how charming.

FALSE FRIENDS

Mr. Zimmons checked in without checking in. He just wanted a key to his room; he didn't want to go through the bother of pulling a credit card out of his skin-tight, powder-blue velvet jeans. He didn't want to waste his time *signing a lot of paperwork and stuff.* He just wanted the key, thank you. I'd only been a desk clerk at the hotel for about three days when he appeared before me, so I questioned the man.

He'd been coming here *for years* he explained with a peculiar mix equal parts saintly forbearance and un-saintly exasperation; he just needed his key, thank you. While he waited, he sighed, rolled his eyes heavenward and threw his entire weight onto one hip. The owner then appeared suddenly, welcomed the gentleman profusely and asked me for the key to the gentleman's room. He would personally show the guest up. (Perhaps he would help him unpack.) "So, how have you been doing, M. Zahmon?" the owner was heard warbling as he carried Mr. Zimmons' bags to the elevator.

In those days, Sylvie and I were not yet married and I called her Miss Bertrand. When Miss Bertrand came into the office I asked her about Zimmons. Her lovely face brightened. Yes, he had been coming here for years. It was a sad story however. This would be the first time Mr. Zimmons had returned since his homosexual companion had died. I brushed that aside and got to the point.
"He didn't check in," I said.
"Oh, I'm sure he'll check in later."

274

"But I didn't get a pre-authorization. I didn't get a deposit. I didn't even get a signature."

My lovely, innocent, fellow office worker, with the cascading tumultuous locks and the somewhat mesmerizing blue eyes, laughed nicely. "He's been coming here for years," she said.

"You know," I said, "it's really none of my business... but there is a reason we take pre-authorizations." I looked her right in those beautiful blue eyes, which I continue to this day to adore.

"It's all right," she consoled me, "Mr. Zimmons has been our guest for years."

As the days ticked by and Mr. Zimmons' bill grew, I nagged the small and lovely Miss Bertrand about trying to obtain some kind of security from the man. In response, she would calmly say, "Mr. Zimmons has been our guest for years."

Meanwhile, our *guest for years* threw an endless string of extravagant parties down in the restaurant and had them all put on his bill. I noticed that there was always a jaw-dropping tip added on, just above Mr. Zimmons' flamboyant signature. I also noticed that the stack of bills attached to his file was getting so thick that our stapler could no longer penetrate it. When I mentioned this to Miss Bertrand, her lovely lips parted and she said, "Mr. Zimmons has many friends and he enjoys entertaining them here." She went on to say that no one consumed wine as eagerly as the guests of Mr. Zimmons (which every bill seemed to confirm) and that it wasn't unusual at all for Mr.

Zimmons himself to arise at one of these events and sing Broadway show tunes, to everyone's delight (which needed no confirmation as far as I was concerned).

I comforted myself by singing "There is nothing like a dame" in my mind for the remainder of the evening.

One evening I felt compelled to talk frankly to Miss Bertrand about Mr. Zimmons. (And, you might someday simply ask my dear wife about this yourself.)

"You know," I said, employing my most sincere, professorial tone, "there are three classic methods scam artists employ for ripping off a small business. Of the employees, there are two distinct types—the stranger with remarkable credentials who shows up suddenly at your door with an almost magical proclivity for bookkeeping, and the long-time devoted employee, who has been screwing you for small amounts regularly, steadily, for years. Third, and this one might be of particular interest to you, is the dedicated client who comes and pays regularly, in order to set you up for that final time when he comes, amasses an impressive bill, and departs in the night. Now, about this Zimmons guy..."

She stopped me with a lovely little lyrical laugh. "Mr. Zimmons has been coming here for years," she said.

"Yes, and that..." I said, "...it's really the classic..."

She laughed again. "Mr. Zimmons has been our guest for years."

When I went to the owner (in those halcyon days we spoke to one another), I expressed these same concerns. He shrugged. He snorted.

He pouted in a distinctly knowing, distinctly French manner, he shook his head. He thanked me somewhat sarcastically for my concern, and said, "This gentleman of whom you speak is a *friend* of ours; he is an old friend of this hotel. He is a FRIEND. He has been coming here for years." He waved to dismiss me. "But, I am sure you don't understand."

I didn't.

But I understood perfectly when, a few days later, that old friend of the hotel, who had been coming here for years, departed suddenly, in the early morning, leaving an enormous unpaid bill behind.

I've been here for more than 12 years now, and we haven't seen or heard from Mr. Zimmons since.
Where are you, old friend?

TRAVEL WRITERS

One of our many self-appointed, walk-in, hotel industry consultants once had the brilliant idea that we should have travel writers stay at our little privately owned hotel for free. And it worked! From the very moment of this idea's inception we were inundated with 'travel writers'. Some stayed three days, some a week, a few stayed longer. The owner was always glad to have them here—giving them a warm welcome, a short talk about the hotel and its history, and a generous free dinner or two, or three or more, including wine. At no point did anyone ask to see their credentials, a tear sheet, a sample of their work. It was, after all, a great honor to have them consider our lovely little hotel as a possible subject for their most honorable and noble craft.

The staff—with one exception—was instructed to treat these travel writers with special consideration. I was purposefully—I'm guessing—left out of the loop, so by the time I heard about this nonsense it had been already going on for some time. I'd been in the presence of travel writers and hadn't even known it.

"Who is this great person staying for a month in 409 and not paying a dime?" I asked a fellow desk clerk one day.
"She is one of the travel writers."
"Travel writers?"
"Yes. The owner has arranged for travel writers to stay here in exchange for writing about the hotel; it costs us nothing!" She sounded quite delighted.
"Well, you get what you pay for," I said.

I was somewhat less delighted than everybody else. And less delighted still when I started looking back through the files and saw that we had already hosted a good half-dozen travel writers. More were slated for the near future.

"How is it that we are so suddenly inundated with travel writers?" I asked.

"The hotel industry consultant suggested it."

"You mean that idiot who lounges around in the owner's office inventing new ways for the hotel to shovel money out the window? The guy with the endless, childish schemes to make this hotel the most desirable destination on earth? The one who struts around here as if he owns the place, and treats all of his friends to perpetual free meals in our restaurant? The one who pats the owner on the back and calls him by his first name? Is that the guy? The guy who treats you like a secretary and me like a servant—that hotel-industry consultant?"

"Yes, Randy."

"Randy, who got us involved in that trade scam in which hundreds and hundreds of people stayed here at no cost whatsoever, while we built up tens of thousands of dollars in trade which we never claimed because the stuff offered in return was absolutely useless? That Randy?"

"We received over $2700 worth of pizza coupons," she said somewhat defensively.

"Yes. That's very good. We put up guests for free and we get pizza coupons. I don't think that is what the hotel business—ultimately, I'm talking ultimately—is about."

"We also have more than $18,000 credit in trade."

"If you want my advice, and I am dead certain you do not—since you didn't ask for it going in," I mumble, "you'll stop this idiocy right now. Take $18,000 in pet pedicures, macramé lessons and psychic readings, put it behind us and try to forget about it."

When I looked up after this nicely crafted little speech, the desk clerk, as dedicated an employee as ever there was, was walking away. But I had more to say.

"Has anyone around here ever asked to see any of the work of any of these so-called travel writers?" I shouted.

This plaintive cry was apparently unheard, or required no answer. But heard or unheard, it demanded a look that might cause any lesser being to wither. I had a file in my hand and I waved it at her. "Errrr!" I said, bringing the matter to an acceptable sort of temporary resolution. If I didn't care, it would all be so much easier.

I went back into the office and began digging up the files on some of the travel writers we had supported in the past. I discovered that, for most of them, no trace of their existence, let alone their work, could be found on the internet. For others there was plenty.

One had written for a woman's magazine which my mother had subscribed to when we were children. In those days it featured stories about husbands who brought home flowers for no reason other than the sudden inspiration (yes, I snorted too), and recipes for jazzing up an apple pie. (The answer was cheddar cheese.) Listed as a contributing editor, our guest's latest contribution had been an article entitled "101 Sex Tricks That Won't Make You Gag". I was sure of two things upon reading this: my mother no longer subscribed to that once staid journal, AND, this

guest was not the kind of travel writer whose work we wanted. At any rate, if this hotel was ever mentioned in any of her future articles, we never heard about it.
She'd stayed for two weeks.

Another travel writer, whose work actually saw print, was a middle-aged woman who wrote for a newsletter distributed within the gated retirement community in which she lived. She proudly sent us a clipping in which the hotel was mentioned. She described us as "a prosaic French island of tranquility, suspended dreamlike in the occasionally tumultuous sea known as *charmingly capricious* San Francisco." In exchange for these kind words she had been given a $135 room for five nights, breakfast daily, and dinner in our relatively expensive, undoubtedly well-respected, always charmingly capricious restaurant, which can be found suspended dreamlike in the bowels of this small, privately owned French hotel. While she compiled facts and worked away slavishly composing that nicely tortured statement, she was—without any doubt—treated like a queen.

I looked up the other frauds and frauds yet to come, and discovered that one of them had actually done a little real travel writing. Several of his articles had been published in a Scottish magazine, with an ale-drinking, soccer-hooligan readership and an actual price on the cover. His most recent article had been "From Fort Lauderdale to Bar Harbor in 72 Hours." Before that he'd written; "NO GUINESS, NO FOOTBALL? Welcome to America!"

Since I seldom speak directly to the owner—such is our unspoken agreement—I told his daughter, to whom I speak frequently, about these so-called travel writers and their output... and she told him... and he shrugged (perhaps), laughed (perhaps), entwined his fingers behind his regal head and smiled knowingly (perhaps)... and soon there was an end to all that travel-writers-stay-for-free nonsense. From that point on, we hosted no travel writers.

On a similar front, we did have a gentleman staying here one time who photographed prairie fires for a living.
"My God," I told him, "that sounds like a cool way to make a buck."
Apparently he did quite well too. He told me as much.
"The shots must be spectacular," I gushed.
He was too humble to admit it.

So, as soon as he left the office I went to his website. I was expecting to be staggered by the images I was about to see. But, I've seen more majestic pictures of sleeping kittens. Those had to be the dullest, most uninspiring photographs ever taken of any prairie fire. In each of them, we look across miles of dry grass in the foreground toward the distant horizon, and there, we think we might detect what appears to be, possibly, a puff or two of smoke.

That gentleman paid his own way at the hotel, so, he wasn't trying to swindle *us*, but, after seeing his work, I knew fraud was certainly living a fairly comfortable existence somewhere in his nature.

A FAIRLY POPULAR MISCONCEPTION

A fairly popular misconception held by a certain select few guests seems to be that you can check into a hotel, go upstairs, screw your girlfriend, or recently acquired drugged-out or drunken acquaintance (if that's all you've got) and then, after spending an hour or two in that room, messing up the bed, using every towel and washcloth in the place, flooding the bathroom floor, scattering potato chip bags, empty beer cans and cheap whiskey bottles around— in short, just generally destroying the place—amble amiably downstairs, yawning and scratching your belly, and declare that you've decided not to stay after all. When asked why, you say the girlfriend doesn't like the color of the room or the pillows are too firm.

When such guests are informed that they must pay for the room, they always bristle. That they are more than welcome to stay the night affords them no comfort: apparently now they've been called back home in an emergency. They are absolutely shocked to think that they might be charged for a room in which they won't be spending the night when their father's cousin's dog needs an appendectomy.

Once they recover from the shock, they make threats; they posture, they demand to know my name (at which point I always fall to my knees, clench my hands together tightly in a humble prayerful manner and, trembling all over, plead for them not to tell my boss). Then they declare, "the owner of this 'kin' joint is going to hear from me!"
(At which point I begin to whimper).

"What's the owner's name?" they demand.
"Harry Heller," I tell them, giving them neither my eyes, my teeth, nor any further attention. Sometimes the owners name is LaFong, Carl LaFong. (Big L, little A, big F, little O, little N, little G, Carl LaFong.)

A kid and his girlfriend checked into the hotel, paid cash, went up to their room and, from the looks of it, wrestled alligators for 45 minutes. After the struggle was over, when they tried to leave the room, the door knob came off in the young male's still-trembling, sweaty palm, trapping them (supposedly) in the room. They called down to the desk. The desk clerk, a college kid, went up and let them out. What they did with the alligators I don't know, but, upon departure they didn't have any more luggage with them than when they arrived, which was none.

She, the one with the tousled bleach-blonde hair and a soft, vibrant glow just below the clavicle, stopped long enough at the front desk to take advantage, in between panting breaths, of the cut crystal bowl which holds a variety of hard candies. He, the one with a smug look upon his unshaven face, stopped only long enough to deposit a door knob upon the desk and turn in the room key. The desk clerk took the opportunity to apologize about the door knob and he said, quote, "That's alright. Don't worry about it." So she didn't.

He returned about two hours later with a somewhat different demeanor, while my wife was at the helm. He started out sweetly, "Maybe you can work with me on this…"

It seems that his girlfriend was frightened to stay at the hotel. That door knob coming off had scared her so thoroughly that she could not possibly force herself to stay at such a horrible place. He demanded a total refund. My wife was confused for the moment, because they had, from every indication, already checked out... as it were. But she was, as she always is, willing to work with him.

Unfortunately for this young man, I am one of those very few select lucky males who not only loves but remains IN love with his wife, and because of that I was hanging around flirting with her when the kid made this ridiculous demand. I chirped up.
"Absolutely not," I said with undeniably cold courtesy.

He looked at me and said, "I wasn't talking to you, I was talking with this lady."

That seemed fair enough. I shut my mouth, crossed my arms upon my chest, and leaned casually against the office furniture—as the security tape would later reveal. My always sweet, naturally kind, perpetually calm, pleasantly unassuming and somewhat innocent wife said, "I'll be glad to offer you another room and, if you need help, we will help you move your things."
"I'm asking you to work with me a little bit on this," said the kid with frustration building in his voice. "My girlfriend is *afraid* to stay here, do you understand? That door knob crap really frightened her. She felt trapped."
"I understand," said my wonderful and always reasonable wife. "But, you have to understand that these things sometimes happen."

He sighed and stared at her, while she continued, "The door knob has been repaired, but, I would be pleased to offer you another room. I'll show you the room I have in mind. Your friend can look at it and see if she feels comfortable in that room."

"I'll look at it," he mumbled.

She handed him a key to another room. He went toward the elevator mumbling something loudly, I could not tell what. My guess: nothing taken directly, word for word, from Emily Post.

When he returned he said that, although it was a nice room, he could not force his girlfriend to stay in a place were she felt uncomfortable and asked, once again, for a complete refund. At this point I spoke up.

"You know," I said, "it doesn't work that way." I carefully avoided using the word, stud, although it came to mind. "You can't come in here, rent a room, *use* the room, check out, come back three hours later, and demand a refund. Now that the room has been used and all of our maids are gone, we can't let it out. My wife has kindly offered you another room. You may stay there, if you choose, until check-out time tomorrow."

I asked for the keys to the room he had just looked at.

"I'm not giving them back until I get my refund," he said.

I said, "You're not getting a refund. As I've already explained, it doesn't work that way. You may stay in either of the rooms that we've offered you, but you're not getting a refund."

By this time my wife was on the phone with the owners of this establishment explaining the situation to them quietly in French.

During this conversation the kid turned to me and said, "You don't know who you're messing with."

I raised one lazy eyebrow in anticipation of hearing who I was messing with, and waited.

"My father might be a high-powered attorney," he said at last, glaring at me.

I showed no sign whatsoever indicating how ridiculous I found that statement. I neither smirked nor did I horselaugh because I couldn't decide which was most appropriate. And I successfully prevented myself from guffawing; for fear that it would lead to bending in two in convulsive laughter. The words "might be" echoed gleefully in my mind.

"And you'll be hearing from him about this," he added, pointing a finger at me.

"I look forward to it," I said brightly. "MY father" I added, "*might be* a high powered-attorney as well. Perhaps the two of them *might* meet in a hypothetical courtroom some day and battle over this highly important matter."

The veins underneath the young man's tattooed horse-like neck began to bulge. "What's your name?" he demanded, and began looking around for a pen and something to write on. "Where's a pen?"

"Edward," I said.

"What's your last name?"

"Here," I said, "take my business card. That'll save you the trouble." I extended a business card in his direction.

"I realize that this is a family run business, but your rudeness is really offensive," he said, "I'm going to write a letter to the owner and tell him…"
"Make it a long one," I said cutting him off inadvertently.
"What?"
"Make it a long letter. Be sure to tell him how your father might be a high-powered attorney. I think he'll appreciate that."
"I'm going to tell him how rude you are."
"It'll be the first time he's ever heard that," I said dryly.
"So, you might want to underline the word *rude* a couple of times."

If that sounds smug that's because I was sick of this kid who thought he could come into our place, fornicate for 17 and a half minutes and depart with a full refund because he ripped the door knob off like a moronic brute on his hormonally charged way out the door.

The long and the short of it was that the too-too-kind owner instructed his daughter over the phone to extract half of what the kid owed and forget about it. Since he had paid cash, my wife began counting out the bills upon the desk.
"CASH!" the kid declared proudly looking at me and pointing at the stuff as my wife counted it out.
I raised my eyebrows in a manner which he correctly took to mean I did not get the point.
"I paid CASH, Chump!" he said, clarifying the point. "I pay cash wherever I go. What does that say to you?"

I did not tell him what it said to me, but, I'll tell you.

What it said to me was some kind of dilettante criminal. By far, most of the people who pay cash in advance at this small, privately owned French hotel are low-lives who cause trouble of one sort or another before they split leaving us with a huge phone bill or broken furniture or a restaurant bill downstairs which they knew, going in, we could never recover. Had I anything to say about it—and I do not—cash in advance would only be accepted in quantities more than sufficient to cover all contingencies. We'll give you your change on the way out, Chump.

"I have more cash on me right now than you will earn in your entire life, Chump!" he continued—raising his chin a bit and staring me in the eye.

I purposefully did not ask him why, if he had so much money, he was wasting so much *time* over a measly 130 bucks. And, I think I deserve credit for my restraint. Still, it was an interesting statement, which required no response, and got none. I mean, maybe he did have more cash on him than I would earn in my entire life. It was certainly possible. In this world it's not unusual at all for the most idiotic and embarrassing people on earth to somehow manage to get ridiculously rich and go around flaunting their bad taste and loudly trumpeting their own stupidity.

Then he said this: "This place is a fire trap. I really should call the fire department."

I was instantly at arms. "Why don't you do that?" I said sharply. "I'll dial the number for you."

Up until that point I had remained relatively calm (cold but calm), relatively civil (stern but civil), and had not raised my voice.

Until that point I had not responded overly to either his insolence or his block-headed, puffed-up, festering arrogance. But this statement got me.

I stood up, I took a step toward him and I said very crisply, "This establishment has been in the same family for more than 40 years. Something like 72% of our guests are returning guests and guest referrals. We don't have to twist any arms to get people to stay here. Our guests come here gladly; they are delighted to stay here. We, in turn, are glad to see them; which separates them from you." Now the veins were standing up on my neck. By this, my own account, I admit I made this statement in what anyone would perceive as a threatening manner.

He was glaring at me in response, and there was a little gap in there so I added, "And our regular guests PAY for their rooms; that's another thing that separates them from you." He continued to glare at me for a bit then said, "You'll be hearing from me," and walked out of the office.
"I can't wait," I shouted loud enough for him to hear me. Odile, I think, would have been proud. My wife was not.

She suggested that, even though I waited for him to get completely outside the front door before I called him a moron, it might have been more professional had I not called him a moron at all. She's probably right: she has had many more years dealing with morons, than I.

KNUIT, WE HARDLY KNEW YE

As said, many guests arrive here with needs which cannot readily be determined; typically they're something of a psychological nature. Some arrive here with an aching need for affirmation of the fact that they are superior to anyone who might be working in a hotel, and position themselves so that they either receive re-affirmation on a continual basis, or go away disgruntled.

But there are real people who show up here with legitimate needs as well. There are at least two middle aged women who walk in from time to time, in clear need of the warmth and comfort and protection that this establishment has to offer, but who do not have every penny of the going rate, whatever it may be at the moment. These poor creatures seem on the verge of homelessness, or perhaps are in fact homeless, but have managed to scrounge enough together for a night's stay out of harm's way. These are good intelligent women who, due to damned circumstance, find themselves in a rough and unforgiving situation, and wish to grab on to what little comfort they can from time to time. I always give them a break, if I possibly can.

It's always heartbreaking when, while walking the dogs, we pass them on the street and they turn away in humiliation, not wishing to be recognized. It's tougher still when one of them shows up here with no money at all, in desperate need, pleading to be given a room, just for the night. I can not tell you what I do in those instances because even when I've done the right thing I don't know if it has truly helped the good woman or not; and, in those times when I can't help, I wonder where my humanity is.

Which leads us to Mr. Knuit.

Mr. Knuit was standing humbly, crumpled hat in hand, before my wife when I came into the office one evening. "The shame that I feel in making this humiliating request can not be adequately expressed, I fear," he was saying. "And the revulsion which you no doubt must most rightly feel may perhaps never be forgiven a stranger. I will understand fully if what I ask of you is anathema to both yourself and your way of doing business." The man was trembling as he spoke. My wife—who had by secret means called me into the office—looked at me sideways as if to say, See what I'm up against?

"What can we do for you?" I demanded loudly, sharply, making my presence known.

"I was just about to embark upon the path which might draw us closer to an answer to that very piquant question. Please forgive me if my manner is somewhat hesitant. The difficulty lies in the fact that, though I am not a proud man, necessity places me in an unfamiliar and uncomfortable position. And I fear that this—my unfamiliarity with…this shameful state in which I now find myself…"

"What is it that you want?" I said.

"Oh. I am so very sorry for taking so much of your valuable time on such an insignificant matter. Please, if you can, in your heart of most sympathetic hearts… forgive me…I will attempt to formulate the nature of my somewhat disgraceful situation in a more expeditious manner."

"I'll take care of this," I told Sylvie, and she got up from her seat behind the desk and departed.

Mr. Knuit was looking anxiously after her as she made her way around the desk, out the door, and down the hall.

"I was… I was …uh… I was presenting my sad case to this lady," he said turning his back to me, craning his neck, hoping for my wife to reappear.

"Yes, and now you are presenting it to me. What can we do for you?"

"It is a somewhat sensitive matter. I had hoped… Could you call the lady back?"

"Talk to me," I commanded. "Have a seat."

"You're too kind. But, I don't wish to take up your time with squalid minutia. I realize that…"

"Have a seat."

"Thank you. That is so very very kind of you. I…"

He sat and looked longingly over his shoulder in the direction in which Sylvie had fled.

"She's gone," I said. "Tell me what it is you want. Do you want a room? Do you want to check in?"

The man did not raise his eyes to meet mine. He fumbled with his hat. I waited. But, I didn't have to wait long. My wife—the woman who loves me despite everything—had gone directly to the owner's office. And now he came into our office and introduced himself as the owner of the hotel and asked the gentleman to come with him. I'm sure the man was relieved. I was. Sylvie came in and thanked me. I thanked her. We rolled our eyes heavenward to thank anyone up there who might have had a hand in getting rid of that guy.

"What do you think he wanted?" she asked.

"Puh! He wants a free room," I said.

The pure coldness that resides in my bitter heart resonated in every syllable. This was not the first time it occurred to me that giving all my love to Sylvie has (perhaps) left me with very little to give to liars, petty crooks, charlatans, salesmen, pig farmers, chicken thieves, and politicians.

Before long, the owner emerged again from his office and came into our office and started wrestling around with the computer in a very convincing manner. Eventually he surrendered and instructed me to find a nice room for the gentleman and to charge him about what a good pair of stolen socks might cost if purloined off a card table in a back alley in Bombay, in 1949. Of course, had the owner not intervened in this matter when he did, this hotel would have been deprived of the honor of having this very fine and excruciatingly humble gentleman occupy a room while he awaited Death's knock upon his door.

That was his story: the man had exhausted his entire fortune trying to maintain his health, and now wanted only to live a quiet little existence until Death overtook him. He had long ago surrendered to the fact that he would never reestablish his previously held, considerably lofty, position in this world; he would never again attain his rightful rank in society or regain his once vibrant health; he could no longer break into joyous song when each new morn brought with its dear dawning rays the glowing hope of true happiness in this Life. So it was that he found himself, regretfully, meekly, humbly, beseeching us to allow him to draw but one time upon the underlying wellspring and the operative creed upon which every hotel throughout the known world has based its business, since time began:

"If your story is good enough, you stay for free."

So, Mr. Knuit moved in, and very soon three things became clear. The first was that you could fit more large plastic bags filled to the brim with who-knows-what in one of our small rooms that one might have supposed. The second was that he enjoyed sitting for prolonged periods opposite either my wife or the owner whenever opportunity reached out, hooked him and dragged him in. The third was that he didn't like talking to me all that much. In fact he didn't like talking to me at all.

His talks with the other two were always overflowing with excruciatingly tortuous humility cast in lengthy meandering sentences that Norman Mailer would have admired. Each little chat was a long drawn out affair that spoke first to the great kindness that he was receiving from us, in his final days here on earth, and then addressed the fact that these were, in all likelihood, his final days here on earth, and concluded with the observation that a quieter room or a sunnier room, or a larger room would really actually, kinda suit him better, you know, in his final days here on earth.

From what I was told, Knuit's regrets were many, but not too numerous to enumerate and describe in every sad detail to anyone who would listen. He once had a dog that was hit by a car... that sort of thing. His talks with me always started out in that manner but never went very far, because he didn't really like me—and he could tell that I could see right through him. So, I never learned the dog's name or what kind of a car it was, though I am sure both my wife and the owner have these facts at their finger-tips.

For all I know there may be a file somewhere around here containing a photograph of the dog as a pup, a note on the license plate number of the car that hit him.

I never gave this gentleman, our guest, the bum's rush, but I did not commiserate with him either. Basically, as I saw it, it was my job to extract the price of 7 pair of shop-lifted socks from him every week, and that is pretty much what I did. I'm not really into manipulation all that much.

Eventually, after the owner had heard every possible permutation of the man's sad tale and long after Sylvie could no longer stand to hear the man's voice (reportedly he was even beginning to give her 'the creeps') these two good and caring people both began to act maybe just a little bit more like me. The owner began to draw his shades at the sound of Knuit's footsteps in the hall—an act which was at once cowardly, wise, and perfectly understandable —Sylvie was always, by chance, just on her way out the door whenever the man showed up.

And, Mr. Knuit was clever enough to get the message; you have to give him credit for that. Almost immediately he shrugged on the dark, heavy, woolen, somewhat tattered, somewhat soiled cloak of persona non grata, and began moving in and out of the hotel silently, swiftly, and only at night. He spoke to no one. If he had anything to say to anyone here, he said it in writing, by far the most favored vehicle for those of us rolling through life on one or more wobbly wheels. For some reason, I alone saw that coming.

"Deeply wounded, I retire…" began one such note.

It ended, as they all did with a meandering paragraph full of regret and the most sincere humble apology for being himself. At this point, *that* was the very thing none of us could find it in our hearts to forgive him for. If his sad tale any longer meant anything to us, we would have to piece it together from mass memory like tribal history, because we sure weren't going to hear it ever again from him. Though he remained in residence, he was, for all intents, a ghost, and ghosts serve no purpose in a small privately-owned French hotel. In time, both my wife and I were having trouble remembering what the man looked like.

"He wore a hat... I think..."

"Or was it a moustache?"

"Yeah, I think you're right. It *was* a mustache."

Where (at what point) in all of this Mr. Knuit stopped paying anything at all for his room, I can not say. But eventually, kind as he is, understanding as he is, the owner could no longer ignore that fact; neither could he ignore the fact that the man wasn't dying at the rate he had originally proposed, nor could he ignore the nagging thought that maybe, just maybe, he wasn't dying at all.

Considering his non-existent efforts, there was little hope that Mr. Knuit would ever again attain the great heights from which he had apparently fallen, and therefore less hope still that he would ever pay his hotel bill. Either way the kindest heart can only stretch so much. And, although I found my indifference pretty much in the same state it had been in when I first barked at the poor lost soul, I knew it would be some time before others came slogging across through the muck of it all, to stand firmly on shore with me.

In general, by the time the owner wants any guest ejected from this hotel it has been crystal clear for a very long time to the rest of us that the guy should have been ejected a long time ago. And so it was with Mr. Knuit. The owner had, for some time, been pretending not to see Knuit whenever he saw him coming, and that had gone on for long enough. Now it was time to take steps to eliminate the possibility entirely. So, it could be said that Knuit's prolonged presence was the owners' impetus for fleeing to France or Greece or wherever people who have both the time and the money go to escape such people.

Word had come down that when they returned Mr. Knuit should no longer be in residence. There was no indication as to how this miracle was to take place, but this misanthrope was pleased to see that his people-handling skills were finally being recognized, albeit indirectly (la honte). Deathly silent as that endorsement might be, the owner knew that I was the only employee up to the task. And, as they went off to bask in the oppressive sun on some ancient blistering, blindingly white island in the middle of the ever-boiling sea, they knew that Mr. Knuit was as good as gone.

Here the adventure really begins, because as I sharpened my teeth in our little rooms Mr. Knuit suddenly took flight one night, leaving all of his things behind.

We, Sylvie and I, didn't really know what to do. Had he died after all? Had he simply run off? It was all very mysterious. And, in California, possessions abandoned in a hotel room have more rights than a fully developed fetus.

From the phone bill I obtained a number which Mr. Knuit had called several dozen times during his stay and I called that number. It turned out to be the local branch of some moldy old fringe of a slowly-dying protestant sect. In fact it was the office of the moldy old bishop himself. I told them I was looking for Mr. Knuit and they asked who I was. I told them I was calling from the hotel, and—CLACK— they hung up.

At this point I pondered:
I'm a basically honest guy. I think everybody who knows me knows that. My wife knows me as a basically honest guy. I think the owners of this establishment know me as a basically honest guy, and probably regret it to some degree. That's both the problem and the cure. In those times when my basic honesty should lead to my praise, it never does; when it should lead to my downfall, it always does. At any rate, because of this basic honesty thing, I theorize that there might be other basically honest people out there, and I knew, from experience, that if you call back any place enough times, eventually you'll stumble, by chance, upon one of them. So, I called up again immediately. We went through those same few dance steps; as soon as I mentioned the hotel—CLACK—they hung up. Being a quick learner I sat out the next few songs.

I don't know what he had told these well-meaning church folk, but whatever it was, it was an outright lie; we had shown this man nothing but kindness. In return, Knuit not only screwed us, but he was going around town begging protection from us…which, if he continued that nonsense, he might soon actually need. So, that kinda bugged me.

Over the next few days, from time to time, at random hours of the day and night, I called that number until, as I'd supposed, I got someone who had not yet been placed in the loop. This poor innocent said, "Oh he's no longer staying here, we've put him up at the Freeling Hotel."
"Thank you," I said.
"When we speak to him, who would you like me to say called?" asked the innocent, and I could hear in his voice the suspicion that he might have spilled the beans.
"A friend," I said. "Tell him *a friend* called." I hung up quickly and called Sylvie to the office that very instant.

I shrugged on my jacket and dashed out the door and flagged down a cab. I sat forward anxiously in my seat as the driver plied his way slowly through heavy afternoon traffic. When we got there, I tossed a bill at the cabbie (just like in the movies) saying —'Thanks. Keep the change' (just like in the movies.) However, un-like in the movies, I didn't call him Bub. I *ran* into the Freeling Hotel, up the grime impacted smelly old carpeted stairs, taking them three at a time, to the front desk. While still huffing and puffing, I asked the enormously overweight woman doing her nails with wafting indifference behind the two inch thick Plexiglas what room Mr. Knuit might be found in.
"Who should I tell him is…"
"A friend," I said. And, even as I said it, I knew I had made a mistake.
The desk clerk looked at me knowingly, and I winced.
I was too late.

The swiftest taxi on earth can't beat a telephone call.

"Is he here?" I asked smiling in a totally unconvincing manner.

"He just stepped out," she said with cool indifference, and looked me right straight, unblinkingly, in the eye.

"OK," I said surrendering to the reality of the situation, "I feel I should advise you about what kind of guy you're dealing with. Mr. Knuit owes us A LOT OF money. You tell him we want his stuff out of the hotel within three days. Three days," I said emphatically. "And, we'd like him to pay his bill." I looked the woman in the eye.

We weighed each other's resolve for a moment, and each found a worthy opponent. But, if there is any single group of people who are not intimidated by me, it is enormously overweight women doing their nails with wafting indifference at the front desk of some dingy old cheap hotel in Chinatown. I don't know when I'll ever learn. She looked both unconcerned and smug as she told me, "Mr. Knuit is a guest of the Holy Innocence Church of Eternal Suffering and they are paying for his stay here. I'll be sure to tell *them* that you've come by... *friend*."

The next day I wrote a nice note to Mr. Knuit saying that he had 72 hours to remove his stuff and return our keys or we'd just throw it all in the garbage. It was an empty threat in the sense that all of that would be illegal... including, probably, the note itself, which I signed with an imaginary flourish. In California if some guest forgets his toothbrush in a room, the hotelier has a legal obligation to protect that precious article until the second generation of heirs of the original owner files written denial to any claim.

On the other hand, Knuit knew me; he knew I was a loose cannon; he had no idea what my limitations were.

That's why I was reviewing the security monitor one morning a couple of days later and came upon the image of Mr. Knuit as he entered the hotel at 3 AM with an emaciated, monkish-looking sort of guy, and gathered up all of his possessions into large black plastic bags.

It took them three trips each, each carrying about what one might load upon a young burro, to remove all of his stuff and get it stacked up outside. For a dying man, he certainly liked his stuff. They then carried it down the block, out of range of our security cameras. Why they would not park directly in front, in our passenger loading zone at that hour, I can not imagine.

When I went up and looked at the room, it was *immaculate*. He still owed us for several thousand pair of cheap knock-off designer socks, and he took our keys with him when he left, but the room was spotless.

Oh the deep wound your departure brings…dear friend… 'haps 't will ne'er heal. Mr. Knuit, we hardly knew ye.

PARTING GIFTS

We have 50 rooms and 60 irons, but none of the irons are IN any of the rooms. Ironing boards can be found in each room and, after our dear guests depart they are all still to be found in the closet. However, for an iron, you have to ask at the front desk. It's understandable because, for years our guests assumed that the irons which we provided in their rooms were parting gifts. I guess they imagine the owner very graciously saying, "You have been such wonderful guests, why don't you take one of these lovely irons with you when you leave? I know you must have one already at home, but this one is newer and, after all, it's free." Where they came up with this idea I do not know, but for many years it seemed to be simply understood. When packing to go home, why not toss in an iron?

So, when a guest needs an iron, they must first spend whatever length of time it takes to convince themselves that there is no iron anywhere in the room, then they must call down and irritably declare, "I found an ironing board, but I can't find the iron.".... as opposed to simply reaching up, taking down the iron from the closet shelf and putting it to immediate use. Then they must wait for me to go get an iron from the maid's closet and bring it to them, as they stand around in their underwear, wondering why. I could, of course, explain why—as I have to you just now—but rarely are they in the mood for it, by the time I arrive and knock upon their door.

Other popular parting gifts seem to be the bathtub plugs—which my wife and I buy by the double fistfuls at regular intervals—and remote controls—which any IDIOT knows work only with the television they come with—and, occasionally, the framed art which hangs in the hallways of this small, privately owned French hotel.

The owner, having had his fill of this particular behavior, once began to compose a terse statement which was to be pasted to the back of every piece of hanging art in the place—all 32,000 of them. Initially the tag was to say something like "CONGRATULATIONS—you have just purchased this fine piece of art. And..." followed by a yet, undetermined blah blah blah. The wording was crucial—of course—and this notice was a work in progress for the better part of several years until it was lost entirely amongst myriad stacks of other vital, on-going, never-ending, ever-emerging concerns the owner of any small, privately owned hotel must face each day. The idea was that we would track the thief back to his room, using our security system, and simply add the cost of the art to his bill. As much as I admired the directness of that approach, there was a flaw. Most of the art that has walked out our door was taken by people other than guests; people who walked in with the sole purpose of lifting art.

It hardly matters. Though our security video captures the very moment such art is removed from the wall, and gets several good pictures of the scoundrel who has taken it, as he makes his way downstairs and out the front door, police have told us such evidence is almost useless to them, and of even lesser use in a court of law. And, I always find it slightly unnerving when the police arrive to 'investigate' the theft and begin their probe by interrogating me.

They do this every time I call to report such a crime. They begin by asking me where I was born, what my middle name is, and how long I've been working here. It usually goes on in that somewhat disturbing manner until I feel compelled to nervously remind them, "I'm the guy who called you."

"We understand that; do you have some objection to answering our questions?"

"No, I just thought I'd mention that to you," I say, punctuated with a nervous laugh.

"Do you find what we're doing here funny?"

"No."

"Are you sure?"

"Yes."

At that point I feel like I'm in a Hitchcock film. From the look in their eyes it becomes clear, once again, that, for reason which I will never understand, cops see me, almost instinctively, as the most likely perpetrator of any crime that has been committed anywhere in my proximity. When I show them a picture of the actual perpetrator, they ask me if I recognize the guy.

Of course, I'm tempted.

"Yep, you got me. Man, I was sure that working here for 14 years was the perfect cover for lifting two mirrors and three small prints."

SECURITY

The security monitors have been helpful many times in tracking down cabs which have scooted off with a guest's possessions. One particularly memorable time a guest got out, placed his laptop up on the roof of the cab, thought better of it, tossed it back inside, and after getting his bags from the trunk, paid the cabbie and came inside as his laptop went for a ride.

Once, while checking in, one of our guests saw the security monitor which showed the street outside and asked, "Do you guys ever witness any accidents on those things?"
I said, "No, you know, we're pretty much focused on what goes on in here; we look at that sort of thing after-the-fact." Even as those words spilled out of my mouth, a car barreled into the rear end of the car stopped directly in front of the hotel. We heard the crash with our own ears; we witnessed the impact with our own eyes, LIVE, as it occurred, from two different angles, on those security monitors.
"Well, that ain't after-the-fact," he said.
"Wow, it sure isn't." I had to agree.
We both ran out to see if anybody needed help.

I'm at the front desk when a guest comes in saying, "I don't know how, but, can you help me? I just left my cell phone in a taxi cab, and I don't even know what cab company it was."
"That's OK," I assure him and I bring up the digital recording of his cab's arrival. I pull it up full frame and see that it's Sullen Cab Company number 403.

"I'll call the cab company," I tell him encouragingly, and start dialing.

"Wait," he says, "Why don't we just call my cell phone and see if someone answers." (This was in the days when cell phones were still fairly rare.)

"THAT," I said, "is one of the loveliest example of clear thinking I've seen in a long while." (This was, in fact, an original thought back then.)

He gives me the number. I dial it. Someone answers sullenly, "Hullo?"

"Is this Sullen Cab number 403?"

"Maybe it is and maybe it isn't, who are you?"

I say, "You just dropped off a fare at our hotel on Bush Street and…"

"I did not," the voice says defiantly.

"Yes," I say sternly, calmly, "you did."

"I wasn't anywhere near there," he says. At this point I put the speakerphone on so our guest can appreciate the wonders of this conversation.

"You deny dropping off a fare at our hotel just a few minutes ago?"

"I haven't been in that area all evening."

"You don't even know what area I'm talking about. But, yes, you were in the area, I have it on our security system. You are driving cab 403; you dropped off our guest here 14 minutes ago; you're wearing some kind of weird white hat."

"Yes," he says, "maybe all of this is true, but I do not have that man's cell phone."

"Yes, you do," I say.

"What makes you think you might be knowing this?" he demands. "How are you even possibly knowing this?"
"Because," I say, "you're speaking on it."
You would think that would be the end of it...
"Maybe this phone is here, but I have just noticed it in the cab only now," he says.
I ask him to bring it by the hotel and he says "OK. But, have the very kind gentleman to meet me out front."

The guest and I are watching the monitor as Sullen Cab #403 pulls up outside a few minutes later. The guest goes out. I'm watching the monitor as the cell phone changes hands and a brief conversation takes place. There's some animated gesticulation from both parties before the guest turns and comes back into the hotel. He stops at the front desk shaking his head in disbelief. "You won't believe this," he says, "The guy wanted a reward!"

Speaking of cabs reminds me of the most predictable thing on earth. If you ever get a chance to bet on this, put everything you have down; your watch, the mortgage, the kids. In the hotel business there are certain things that are always predictable, but none more predictable than this; it happens 100 percent of the time, if not more.

If someone asks me to call a cab for them, I always make them promise to have a seat in the lobby and wait there until that cab arrives. But, they will not sit in the lobby and they will not wait until that cab arrives. They will promise to. But, they won't. As soon as I get off the phone with the cab company, I'll look up to see that person, who has just promised to sit in the lobby, exiting the front door.

Then, on the monitor, I'll then watch as they step into the street and raise their hand. But there is nothing anyone can do about it. By the time I run out the front door, they're already in the back seat and the cab is pulling away. The best anyone might do, if you're very quick and extremely agile, is to attempt to put a dent in the trunk of the cab as it drives off—injuring your fist in the process—and that's sending the wrong message to the wrong recipient. Besides, cabbies must be used to that sort of thing.

The ONLY people who EVER have asked me to call them a cab, and have promised to wait in the lobby, and *have then actually done that*, are crippled by old age or injury or both. And, of the many people asking me to call them a cab, who I've told about this phenomenon, only two have stuck around—I suppose to make a point. With the exception of those two, no person who is not physically immobilized has ever been here when the cab that I've called *at their request* arrives, not one. The very real question then arises, how long did I continue to participate in this ridiculous and irritating charade before I finally learned my lesson? Or, more precisely, at what point did I start picking up the phone just as though I was actually going to call a cab company?

If you're charting this, don't forget to factor in the irrefutable fact that cab drivers HATE going to a hotel only to discover that the fare is no longer there. They certainly have good reason.

Because of this, for a very long time I was convinced that I knew how my life would end.

Naturally, my killer would not be in the mood to listen to my plea; he probably wouldn't have time to consider how I had, through the years, begged and pleaded and insisted and demanded, ordered and cajoled, and tried, in every way possible, to manipulate each and every one of those people into sitting down in the goddamned lobby and waiting for the goddamned cab like they had goddamned promised me they would. Dear God in Heaven I have tried. I have tried. I have tried. I have tried. I made every single blasted one of them promise me that they would stay. None did.

That's why your fare is not here, Mr. Cab driver. Please, lower your gun. Consider this: I was a cab driver myself in this town not so very long ago.

BLIND RAGE

Here's a charming little tale, unfortunately true, which everyone seems to enjoy.

When the party of 26—mostly blind—guests arrived, they were all loud, they were all demanding, and apparently from their behavior they were all drunk. They crammed seven people onto an elevator which holds four, and by forcing the inner gate open and closed, and by pushing every available button, managed to break the elevator.

During their entrapment, while riding up and down, they were screaming and laughing raucously, absolutely delighted that they had broken the thing. Once they were all downstairs in the restaurant and seated, they proved to be loud, crude and vulgar. Two couples—guests of the hotel—came to me at the front desk and said they were sorry but they could not eat down there. One guest said that it was "unbearable". The Chef told me later that the blind people were not just drunk but exceedingly drunk; some had thrown up in their plates, for god's sake, some had fallen off their chairs… all to the great amusement of the others.

One of the blind gentlemen fell down on his way to the men's room and the pastry chef called me to come down and offer him help. So, I locked up quickly and went downstairs to see what I could do. There, I saw the man lying on his back just outside the door to the restaurant. He was surrounded by three other blind men, two with white canes and one with thick dark glasses. They were comforting him and telling him to just lie there for a while.

I observed him carefully. He was conscious and speaking to his attendant friends, and he expressed no pain when they assisted him up to a sitting position on the floor. I asked, "Would you like me to call for an ambulance?" and was told, "No; he'll be OK." I made my way around the gathering and went into the restaurant and got a chair for the man to sit on, so they could get him up off the floor. When I returned one of them with a white cane turned to me and commanded, "You lift him, I can't," and abandoned the scene. I helped the others get the man up and seated on the chair. Then I went into the kitchen to call Sylvie and tell her she should go in and attend the front desk while I watched over things downstairs.

When I came back out of the kitchen, I asked, "Is he going to be OK?" and the man with the dark glasses turned to me and said, "Get us a cab! I want a cab right out there." He pointed toward the basement.
I said, "I'll get a cab for you, but it'll be upstairs."
He approached me and put his hand on my chest. "Are you listening to me?" he said, "I want a fucking taxi *down here*, not up stairs. I want it right outside that door," he said, pointing once again into the basement, "and I want it now!"

I said. "There's no exit on this level…" and that man stepped up to me and, with his face within inches of mine, said, "Listen to me very closely. Are you listening to me? I want a fucking taxicab, right now, and I want it right there, outside that door." And he pointed again to the basement. "But, I can't get a taxi…" I started to explain. Then this guy put both hands on my chest and he shoved me so hard I almost fell over backward.

I said, "Don't put your hands on me."
He came up to me, put his face to within four inches of mine and he said, "Listen very carefully to me. Are you listening? I'm not so sure you are…" and he put both of his hands on my chest and shoved me again.

Let me tell you something. I have never struck another human being in my entire life, but, had I not been representing this establishment at that moment, he would have been the first. I like to think that I would have hit that goddamned stupid moron as hard as I possibly could, right squarely in the nose, with every hope of breaking it—blind or not. Instead I said, "Don't put your hands on me again or I'll have you arrested."
"Have me arrested?" He laughed derisively and said, "You faggot…"
At this point I retreated into the kitchen and the man pursued me. When he started to reach for me again, I repeated, "Do NOT put your hands on me again or I will have you arrested." At this point the chef came out of the kitchen and stood beside me, and the man backed off.
I then went upstairs and called a cab.

When this drunken band of utter disgrace was leaving, this same guy intentionally passed by me very closely and muttered, "Faggot."
I said, "If you ever touch me again I'll have you behind bars." As they were leaving through the front door he was very loudly, very proudly, spitting out vitriol.
"No wonder they call it San-fuckin-faggot-frisco." And "Here the faggots fuck like dogs on the sidewalk."

Sylvie said to me, "I didn't know what to expect from a party of blind people, but I certainly never expected that." I was so furious that I could do nothing but pace back and forth between the office and the lobby. I paced like a caged animal for ten minutes.

While I was pacing around suffused with rage—a nicely dressed couple, a small gentleman and a tiny old blind woman, stopped in front of me. She was almost in tears. "I'm so sorry," she said.

"No, no, Madame, it's not your doing." I said. "We know that."

"But it just gives such a bad impression of the entire blind community. I'm so embarrassed by everything that happened here this evening."

"No-no, please, it's OK."

"But, I'm so very sorry. It gives such a bad impression. We're not that way. Blind people are not like this."

"Please, Madame," I said, "don't be concerned."

"We're not all like that… Oh, I'm so sorry," she said and she put her hand gently upon my arm.

"Please, Madame," I said touching her shoulder, "We understand. And, it's OK."

So, I don't know what the moral of this tale might be. And I don't know why that stupid bastard thought he could get away with putting his hands on me; I have over thirty years of disappointment stored in my right fist alone. So, I don't know how I managed to stand there and take it.

But, I do know this:
I hope that son-of-a-bitch gets run over by a bread truck.

A METAPHOR (nothing more)

A guy walks in off the street, comes into the office, shoots me in the head and goes running out again. The owner comes dashing in and says, "What have you done?!"

I'm stunned, I'm in shock. I'm on the floor, sitting in a slowly-expanding pool of my own blood. "Huh…?"
"What have you done to turn away this guest?" he demands.
"He was not a guest," I say.
"No? But, there you are wrong."
"He was NOT a guest," I insist, while applying pressure to my wound.
"Everyone who comes through our door is our guest. Even before, even before… but you do not see this… you cannot see this… you will never see this."
"He shot me in the head," I whine.
"Well then, you must ask yourself what you have done to generate in him this violent reaction. Did you welcome him warmly?"
"I did not have time to welcome him warmly. He came in, he shot me in the head, and he left."
"Oh, that is just an excuse. Well, I suppose we will never see him again…"
"I suppose we won't."
"And that is a shame, he might have become a good customer, a steady customer; a guest in our restaurant. He may have invited his friends. He may have become a greatly honored guest, but you, you do not welcome him warmly. No, you refuse to welcome him in a proper manner, and now he is gone."

"I don't think he would have made a good customer."
"Oh, how can you say that? You don't know this gentleman."

He sighs the sigh of 10,000 martyrs. He looks at me for a very long time. He rubs his tired eyes. The futility of what he is about to do is crushing. He sighs deeply again preparing himself to offer instruction that he has offered me SO many weary times before.
"When there is a *guest* standing before you, you must look up from what you are doing and you must welcome him *warmly*. You must smile. You must invite him to sit down. But with you there is no smile, no bonjour. Perhaps this is why he has shot you, non?"
"Look," I start to respond, "the guy..."
"Pah! Now he has run off. You should think about how you have treated this man... a fine gentleman who could have been our guest."

But, I don't have to think about it. Without giving the matter a single thought, I know that I will never see the owner's point.

And, for that, of course, I should be hung.

☐

An actual review: "I didn't care for the coldness of the staff. Also, there was no air conditioning in the room, no ice bucket, and no fridge."

Books available from Estuary Publications

WHEN I WAS A LOW-LIFE: An American Education by Henry Edward Fool The culmination of nearly 50 years of writing, as well as occasional thought, concerning 4 college years in Richmond, Virginia, beginning 1967

TRIAL BY GUEST: An Accurate Accounting of the Various Reasons I Should Be Hung by Henry Edward Fool Concerning 12 years working in a small privately owned French Hotel, in San Francisco, beginning 1999

AMERICAN RACONTEUR: Real American Writin' for Real American Readin' by Henry Edward Fool Excerpts from the blog of that same title, concerning the 18 years prior to, and the nearly 40 years after the events recorded in *Low-Life*

LOST IN THE DIN: Why Your Opinion on Politics and Religion Means NOTHING, and Mine Means Even Less by Henry Edward Fool Concerning politics as seen from an a-political POV

REFINEMENT: How a Good Marriage Can Nudge an Unwary Man in the Direction of Civility by Henry Edward Fool Concerning marriage

AWAKE AMID ANCESTRAL DREAMS poetry by Emma Moonsinger

WORDS FOR THIS CANNOT BE FOUND poetry by H. Edward Fool

EARWIG, also includes Jack Nicholson IS Santa Claus, 2 short stories adapted from screenplays by Darryl Mockridge

TWO WEEKS in BLÉTANTE by Darryl Mockridge (FICTION)

RETURN to BLÉTANTE by Darryl Mockridge (FICTION)

WHY GOD GAVE US GUNS by Darryl Mockridge (Short Stories)

Made in the USA
Coppell, TX
16 January 2026

67686477R00177